A BRIEF HISTORY
OF THE PRESBYTERIANS

A BRIEF
HISTORY OF THE
PRESBYTERIANS

James H. Smylie

Geneva Press
Louisville, Kentucky

Book and cover design by Jennifer K. Cox

First edition

Published by Geneva Press
Louisville, Kentucky

This book is printed on acid-free paper that meets the American National Standards Institute Z39.48 standard. ♾

PRINTED IN THE UNITED STATES OF AMERICA

96 97 98 99 00 01 02 03 04 05 — 10 9 8 7 6 5 4 3 2 1

Library of Congress Cataloging-in-Publication Data

Smylie, James H. (James Hutchinson), date.
    A brief history of the Presbyterians / by James H. Smylie — 1st ed.
      p.   cm.
    Includes bibliographical references and index.
    ISBN 0-664-50001-3 (alk. paper)
    1. Presbyterian Church—United States—History.   2. Presbyterian Church—History.
I. Title.
BX8935.S56   1996
285'.173—dc20   96-24458

CONTENTS

91473

PREFACE

Dr. Lefferts A. Loetscher, professor of American Church History at Princeton Theological Seminary, wrote *A Brief History of the Presbyterians* in 1938. It proved so useful in introducing readers, clergy, and laity to the subject that the author was asked to revise and update it twice before his death in 1981. In recent years, the Reverend George Laird Hunt contributed a chapter, in the fourth edition, on the union of the United Presbyterian Church in the United States of America and the Presbyterian Church in the United States.

This book, while remaining faithful to the spirit of Loetscher's work, contains fresh dimensions on the Presbyterian story. Its purpose is to provide a brief, accessible, celebrative but not uncritical, presentation of Presbyterian faith and life. This treatment sets the stage by reviewing the origins of the Christian family in the ancient world, as well as the Reformed tradition in Europe and Great Britain. It concentrates on various Presbyterian denominations in the United States of America in the context of the development of a worldwide Christian family. The study touches on major emphases in worship, theology, and governance, as well as on the Presbyterian concern for evangelism, education, mission, and the pursuit of the public good. Moreover, the book incorporates insights from studies about ecumenics and laity, women, and minority groups that have played important roles in Presbyterian history. The persons and groups referred to by name in these pages represent only a small number of a great cloud of witnesses who have tried to live by faith, hope, and love as Christians who happen to be Presbyterians.

This volume is dedicated to Lefferts A. Loetscher, an admired mentor and friend. I offer deep appreciation to my dear wife, Elizabeth Roblee Smylie, for reading the manuscript and also making numerous valuable suggestions. She also put up with me as I worked on this project. I give thinks to Kathy Davis and Jill Torbett of Union Theological Seminary in Virginia who first prepared this manuscript for publication.

I also wish to express appreciation to Professor Charles M. Swe

Union Theological Seminary, Virginia, who read the manuscript with care and improved it greatly. I also thank Davis Perkins, President/Publisher, and Lorene K. Johnson, Production Editor, of Presbyterian Publishing Corporation for their many valuable suggestions and for seeing it through the press.

This text is offered to the reader with faith and hope that the Christ of the Emmaus road may accompany us, and may open our eyes to the Scriptures, to the history of the "one, holy, catholic, and apostolic" church, and to the Presbyterian tradition. May all Presbyterians be instructed, corrected, and also inspired on our own pilgrimages to love one another and the world for which Christ gave of himself.

1

From the Acts of the Apostles to the Age of the Reformation

Presbyterians from the beginning have always claimed to be a part of the whole Christian family. They have confessed belief in the "one, holy, catholic, and apostolic church," stretching back through the ages and now extending around the world. They have recognized their history as a part of this larger community of believers, not only of the apostolic age, but also all of the intervening centuries, especially those of the Protestant Reformation. Presbyterians have stated this in "A Declaration of Faith," produced in 1976 by the Presbyterian Church in the United States, which is an expression of Christian faith and life widely used in Presbyterian worship. It recounts:

> The church's story with God did not end
> with the latest events recorded in Scripture.
> Across the centuries the company of believers
> has continued its pilgrimage with the Lord of history.
> It is a record of faith and faithlessness, the glory and shame.
> The church has been persecuted by hostile societies,
> but it has also known times of privilege and power
> when it joined forces with dominant cultures.
> It has sought holiness
> through separation from society,
> as well as through involvement in the world's affairs.
> It has experienced life-giving reformations.
> It has known missionary expansion throughout the world,
> but also periods of dwindling resources and influence.
> It has divided into rival orders, sects and denominations,
> but it has also labored for cooperation and union.
> We confess we are heirs of this whole story.

We are charged to remember our past,
to be warned and encouraged by it,
but not to live it again.
Now is the time of our testing
as God's story with the church moves forward through us.
We are called to live now as God's servants
in the service of people everywhere.

In the spirit of this "Declaration," the story begins. This book is a brief history of the Presbyterians. More specifically, it is a brief history of American Presbyterians, focusing on the stories of major American denominations—the Presbyterian Church in the United States of America (PCUSA/ 1788), the Cumberland Presbyterian Church (CPC/1810), the United Presbyterian Church in North America (UPCNA/1858), the Presbyterian Church in the United States (PCUS/1861), the United Presbyterian Church in the United States of America (UPCUSA/1958), the Presbyterian Church (U.S.A./1983), and some smaller denominations that identify themselves with this tradition. The recitation of these names and dates tells a story of division, reunion, and union that will be a major part of this history. The history begins, however, with the period from the "Acts of the Apostles to the Age of the Reformation," and then explores the Reformed tradition as it took shape during the Protestant Reformation in Europe and the British Isles. The story finally leads to what is now the United States of America. This past is not dead. It still touches present-day worship, theology, governance, and concern for public life. As William Faulkner once wrote, the past "is not even past." This chapter serves as a prologue to the brief history of Presbyterianism, providing not only information, insight, and inspiration but also a perspective for facing present-day challenges.

From the Acts of the Apostles
to Constantine the Great

Today began a long time ago. The early Christian community grew from small beginnings in the first century of what is known as the Christian era. The community grew until it became the dominant and official religion of the Emperor Constantine and the Roman Empire. Jesus, according to Christians, appeared in the "fulness of time" in the Greco-Roman world. Philip and Alexander had conquered and spread Hellenic culture and philosophy through the then-known world. Greeks and others who gathered in the Acropolis in Athens acknowledged numerous deities, even raising a standard to an "Unknown God" to cover all life's possibilities. Roman Caesars conquered Greece, expanded the empire, and bound it together with law and technology, including its remarkable, inter-empire highway system, which made it easier for Jesus' disciples to spread their message. Romans erected the Pantheon in Rome—a temple for all the gods. The emperors were included among the gods, representing a piety that unified the various factions of the empire. The importance of the Christian community may be measured by the fact that around the year 550 the Greeks and the Romans considered the years from the birth of Jesus, as Anno Domini, A.D. the year of the Lord.

Jesus conquered the Greek and Roman worlds. Christians believed in Jesus as Immanuel—God with us. They remembered Jesus as a Palestinian Jew, heir to the Hebrew traditions about Adam and Eve, Cain and Abel, Abraham and Sarah, Jacob and Rachel, Isaac and Rebecca, Moses and Miriam. He was heir of David and Bathsheba, Solomon and Job and their wisdom. He was heir of the prophets Elijah, Isaiah, Jeremiah, Amos, and Daniel. According to followers, he was the "hope of Israel." Disciples also remembered the morning star, the angel chorus, Jesus' lowly birth, and the "Magnificat" of Mary, the "Benedictus" of Zechariah, and the "Nunc Dimittis" of Simeon. They remembered his early childhood, his baptism by John, his temptations in the wilderness. They remembered that he came preaching.

> The time is fulfilled, and the kingdom of God has come near; repent, and believe in the good news. (Mark 1:15)

as well as,

> The Spirit of the Lord is upon me,
>   because he has anointed me to bring good news to the poor.
> He has sent me to proclaim release to the captives
>   and recovery of sight to the blind,
>   to let the opposed go free,
> to proclaim the year of the Lord's favor.
>   (Luke 4:18; see also Isa. 58:6; 61:1–2)

His followers remembered Jesus' calling the twelve disciples: Simon Peter, Andrew, James the son of Zebedee, John, Philip, Bartholomew, Thomas, Matthew, James the son of Alphaeus, Thaddaeus, Simon the Zealot, and Judas Iscariot. They remembered his parables, the Sermons on the Mount and on the Plains, and the prayer of the Kingdom of God:

> Our Father in heaven,
>   hallowed be your name.
> Your kingdom come.

Your will be done, on earth as it is in heaven.
Give us this day our daily bread.
And forgive us our debts, as we also have forgiven our debtors.
And do not bring us to the time of trial,
but rescue us from the evil one.

(Matt. 6:9–13)

The early Christians remembered Jesus as healer, as well as the one who pronounced forgiveness of sins. They remembered his cleansing the Temple, and his Last Supper in the upper room, where he celebrated the Passover with his disciples. They remembered his trial by religious and political authorities and his words from the cross: "Father, forgive them; for they do not know what they are doing" (Luke 23:34). They remembered the empty tomb and his resurrection appearances that made their hearts burn within them, reviving their faith and hope and love. They remembered many things. And they also remembered Jesus' giving them a great commandment of love and a "Great Commission" to proclaim the good news of God's love and to baptize all "nations" into that love in his name.

The Acts of the Apostles begins with the story of Pentecost—The Holy Spirit moved in Jerusalem among a great crowd of multiethnic people and caused them to hear Peter preaching the message of Jesus in their own languages. Although some thought these people were drunk, the converts became among the earliest members of the Christian family. One of the first things the community did was to minister to those in need, appointing persons as deacons to serve those needs: Stephen, Philip, Prochorus, Nicanor, Timon, Parmenas, and Nicolaus. Later, Paul, a "Pharisee of the Pharisees," persecuted those early Christians until he encountered Jesus on the Damascus road and was converted. He then became an "Apostle to the Gentiles" as well as to the Jews. He proclaimed in his letter to the congregation of Christians in Rome: The just shall live by the grace of God and by faith in that love alone. He preached Christ, crucified for the sins of the world, a belief which was considered by the Greeks as foolish and by the Jews as scandalous. He preached Christ risen, the victor over death (the last enemy of human life). People heard his message.

Women, including Mary the mother of Jesus, and Mary Magdalene— who followed Jesus even to the cross—spread the Good News in both words and works. Dorcas was known for her generosity. Lois, who educated Timothy in the faith, and her daughter Eunice, built up the body of Christ. Lydia, a noble woman, opened her heart and home to Paul, nurturing the growing Christian community.

The church spread east into Persia and India, west to Rome and Spain, south to Egypt, Ethiopia, and across northern Africa, and north into Gaul and Germany, and to the British Isles as early as the fifth century. Patrick, apostle and patron saint of Ireland in the fifth century A.D., left us evidence of the deep piety of the Irish:

> Christ be with me, Christ within me,
> Christ behind me, Christ before me,
> Christ beside me, Christ to win me
> Christ to comfort and restore me,
> Christ beneath me, Christ above me,
> Christ in quiet, Christ in danger,
> Christ in hearts of all that love me,
> Christ in mouth of friend and stranger.
> (*Book of Common Worship*, 27).

As the Christian community grew, its organization expanded under councils held in regional centers. The churches were presided over by bishops and elders (terms sometimes used interchangeably). Deacons served as church officers. The rulers of the empire considered Christians to be atheists because they would not worship pagan gods, including the emperor, to whom the law required them to burn incense. Christians were persecuted intermittently, sometimes harshly, especially under Emperor Nero. In the face of such persecution, John wrote the book of Revelation, setting down his vision of a "new heaven and a new earth."

Many Christians became martyrs to the faith. Polycarp, bishop of Smyrna, a link to the apostolic age, was arrested and ordered to repudiate Christ. He replied: "For eighty-six years I have been serving him, and he has done me no wrong. How then can I blaspheme my King who has saved me?" The Romans burned him at the stake. The martyrs' blood has been called the "seed" of early church growth. Their bones, and other relics of the early church, were widely cherished as having miraculous healing power. Christians, including both Jewish and Gentile converts to the new community, became a "Third Force" in the empire.

During one of the bloody struggles for control of the empire, Constantine claimed to have seen a vision of the cross bearing the inscription: "In this sign, conquer." This dates his conversion to Christianity and his many military victories. In the Edict of Milan of 313, he ended official persecution of Christians. However, he still tolerated other religions under his rule. The Edict was an important step in the final establishment of Christianity as the religion of the empire under Theodosius. Constantine built many churches throughout his domain. He also moved the capital from Rome to Constantinople, now considered the second Rome. In the eastern part of the church he is revered as the thirteenth apostle. In the case of civil magistrates, Jesus taught his disciples to give to Caesar what belonged to Caesar and to God what belonged to God. Paul also admonished Christians to respect the civil magistrate as a gift of God to encourage good and curb evil in the world. But the early disciples also believed that they must obey God rather than civil authorities. Although the emperor still was the most powerful force in the empire, Christians would not sacrifice to him. Rather, they reminded him of his responsibility and accountability to God. They prayed *for* him, not *to* him, thus helping bring about a decisive change in political relationships during those early Christian years.

From the Age of Constantine
to the Age of Reformation

Between the fourth and fifteenth centuries, many events and developments took place that still influence today the way Christians worship, confess the faith, govern themselves, and relate to the world. For instance, when Constantine moved the capital of the empire from Rome to Constantinople, he contributed further to the division between the western Roman Catholic and eastern Orthodox churches, as they came to be called. Then, in 410, Germanic tribes led by Alaric fought their way south and captured and sacked Rome—considered the Eternal City. The event shocked the world. Later, in the seventh century, Islam, led by the prophet Muhammad, spread across Africa into Spain, then into eastern Europe, finally conquering Constantinople in 1453. Islam even threatened Vienna on the eve of Reformation. As these military-political events took place, Christians adopted the canon of the Bible as the norm of Christian faith and life, developed their patterns of worship, creeds and theology, structures of governance, and ways of relating to the world as followers of Jesus.

The Christian community began early to cherish and gather writings about Jesus and his person and work. Previously, Jews had collected Hebrew Scriptures, along with some Hellenic Jewish writings that some Jews considered the Apocrypha. These Scriptures were called the canon—part of the authoritative measure of Hebrew faith and life. Christians accepted the Hebrew canon as their own, with reservations about the apocryphal books, adding the four Gospels and the thirteen letters attributed to Paul, about the year 130. They still debated the canonicity of other books and letters. The canon was finally adopted by a church council, which was probably held in Rome, in 382. The Christian community still uses this canon.

Jerome, a Roman convert to Christianity, emerged as one of the most important early interpreters of the Bible. After his conversion, he became a hermit in Syria and learned Hebrew. He then returned to Rome, where he studied and became a great scholar of the church. He was supported and assisted while in Rome by a number of noble women, notably Marcella, who also studied the Scriptures and exchanged with Jerome philological ideas, thus sharpening his own biblical consciousness. Jerome then moved to Bethlehem, where he wrote biblical commentaries and translated most of the Bible from the original tongues into Latin in a version still known and used in the Roman Catholic Church—the Vulgate. When Alaric sacked Rome, Marcella was maltreated by the invaders and as a result died shortly thereafter. When Jerome heard echoes in the Middle East of Rome's disaster, he groaned, "What is safe if Rome perishes?"

During those years, Christians developed the main forms of worship, both in the east and the west. At first Christians worshiped simply, sometimes in synagogues, sometimes secretly in catacombs. According to early records, worship included the reading of Hebrew Scriptures, Christian writings, preaching, prayer, singing, Baptism, and the Lord's Supper. Christians usually worshiped on Sunday, rather than on Saturday, celebrating the day of resurrection the first day of the week. Over the years, the liturgical calendar grew to include Easter, the most important day of the year, with Lent as a time of preparation. Pentecost became a celebration of the outpouring of the Holy Spirit. Christians began to observe Christmas around the time of Constantine. As the church grew in influence, affluence, and power, the liturgy became more and more structured and elaborate, as can be seen in the Liturgies of Jerusalem, of Alexandria, and in the great "Liturgy of St. John Chrysostom," named for one of the great preachers in the early church. Emperor Justinian built the great church of Hagia Sophia (Holy Wisdom) in Constantinople, making it fit for the capital of the empire and royal worship. The magnificent dome signified the meeting of heaven and earth in worship, as well as the great victory of God in Christ over the decay, destruction, and death of this world. The patterns of worship in the west also grew more complex, similar to those developments in the east. Although not neglecting the hope in the resurrection, the west placed greater emphasis on the suffering and death of Christ for the sins of the world.

Eastern Christians tended to think of all life as sacramental, that is, a sign and a seal of God's love for the world. However, western Christians focused on what became the seven sacraments, covering passages of this life: Baptism of infants (and adults), Confirmation, the Eucharist, Penance, Anointing of the sick (which became Extreme Unction), Ordination to the priesthood, and Marriage. The western church held that Christ was present at the Sacrament of the Lord's Supper, in the bread and wine, miraculously changed by the Holy Spirit into the body and blood of the Savior. The sacramental system gave church leaders enormous authority and power. It was subject to abuse, as is all human power. As in the east, with its Byzantine structures, in the west, worshipers experienced awe in the great Romanesque and Gothic cathedrals with their arches, altars, and fonts. The technology of the flying buttresses made possible the soaring naves and the stained-glass windows that not only inspired worshipers but educated them about the Bible and the traditions of the church. An iconography controversy in the eighth and ninth centuries focused attention on images for religious purposes and the potential danger of idolatry in their use. The Orthodox were more concerned about this than were the western Christians, a difference that further divided the church. The music, such as Gregorian chants, also enriched the liturgies. The architectural arrangements of the great churches in the east and the west magnified the growing separation and distance of priests from other people during those centuries.

Early Christians faced intellectual challenges of the Greco-Roman world, and some were reluctant to engage in a dialogue with non-Christians. "What has Jerusalem to do with Athens?" Tertullian asked, although he was himself a formidable apologist for the faith. Early Christians confessed a simple faith in Jesus as Lord. Gradually, using Hebrew and Christian Scriptures and insights from the Gentile world, they began to write theology and formulate creedal statements summarizing their beliefs about God and the nature and destiny of God's creation and creatures. Being monotheists, they opposed polytheism (belief in many gods) and pantheism (which identifies the universe with god). At the same time, they confessed God's relations through Jesus Christ and the Holy Spirit. They did this in the Apostles' Creed, focusing on the Triune ascriptions of the Bible. This creed was used early, but not given a title until about 390 A.D. It reads (Ecumenical version):

> I believe in God, the Father almighty,
>   creator of heaven and earth.
> I believe in Jesus Christ, God's only Son, our Lord,
>   who was conceived by the Holy Spirit,
>   born of the Virgin Mary,
>   suffered under Pontius Pilate,
>   was crucified, died, and was buried;
>   he descended to the dead.
>   On the third day he rose again;

he ascended into heaven,
he is seated at the right hand of the Father,
and he will come to judge the living and the dead.
I believe in the Holy Spirit,
the holy catholic church,
the communion of saints,
the forgiveness of sins,
the resurrection of the body,
and the life everlasting. Amen.

As the church took root in Hellenic soil, Christians further refined the mystery of the relation between the Father, Son, and Holy Spirit in philosophical terms at the Councils of Nicaea (325) and Chalcedon (451). The Christian community wisely placed the Nicene Creed within the liturgy of the church, emphasizing that God's nature and ways are mysterious, and cannot be encapsuled in a dogmatic formula. The divine-human encounter takes place with God, One in three persons, God transcendent yet with us and for us.

The Christian community produced a number of great theologians, among them Augustine of Hippo. Augustine (354–430), whose father was a pagan, was raised by a Christian mother, Monica. Born in North Africa, he turned from the Christian faith of his youth to study rhetoric, law, and philosophy. While in Milan under the influence of Bishop Ambrose, he returned to the Christian community, and later was consecrated a bishop of Hippo. In his autobiographical work, *Confessions,* about his experience of redemption from sin, he credits his mother and her persistent prayers for his conversion. He confessed to God: "You have formed us for yourself and our hearts are restless until they find rest in you." In other works, he gave considerable attention to doctrine: for example, *The Trinity,* in which he developed a psychological analogue of knowing and loving to explore God's nature. In the *City of God* (413–26), he responded to the panic of persons like Jerome about the sack of Rome, and also to the accusation of pagans that Christians had caused this trauma to the empire. Christians hope in God, he wrote, not in the empire. In this work, Augustine also offered the first major theology of history for Christians, by describing God's sovereignty over all human affairs as a continuous, dynamic relationship between the city of the earth and the City of God. Such a view involved judgment, as well as the promise of the final fulfillment of God's purposes for all creation embraced in both time and space. He also described the Christian community as an instrument responsible for witnessing to God, who was made known to the world through Jesus Christ and the witness of the Holy Spirit. Through his biblical commentaries and theological works, Augustine made a lasting impact that is still felt in the Christian community. Thomas Aquinas and, later, Martin Luther and John Calvin widened his influence through their writings. Monasteries preserved this knowledge, and out of these orders arose great universities.

In much the same manner, the way Christians governed themselves grew more complex as century succeeded century. This was true especially with the establishment of the Christian faith as the religion of the empire and as the church assumed greater responsibilities for its rulers and citizens. As already indicated, the earliest community involved a simple structure of church councils led by bishops, elders, and deacons, who had oversight over the whole church, including the care of the poor and needy. Episcopal authority and power grew as those who held that office emerged as apologists and defenders of the community. To be under the rule of a bishop became a test as to whether a believer was in the "one, holy, catholic, and apostolic" church. In the east, the patriarch of Constantinople emerged as equal with other patriarchs of the various Christian churches of that area. In the west, the pope of Rome, considered himself the successor of Peter and ruler of the See of Peter. He emerged as the central figure who, like the patriarch, governed an increasingly complex hierarchical and bureaucratic system with its numerous offices and personnel. Women such as Marcella were not only patrons, but rendered valuable service to the church in those years. They had less to do with the formal government of the church, however.

Pope Leo III presided in Rome over the coronation of Charlemagne the Great, on Christmas Day, 800, as emperor of the Holy Roman Empire. The tension between the east and west increased. The event also enhanced the authority and power of the pope, who governed a sacramental system necessary for the salvation of emperor and people. The interests of the church and the temporal authorities often conflicted. Ambrose of Milan, a bishop, insisted that Emperor Theodosius do penance for a military massacre. When Pope Gregory VII was opposed by Henry IV, as the former attempted to reform the church, Gregory excommunicated the emperor and released his subjects from their allegiance to him. Henry stood for three days in the snow at Canossa, waiting for the pope's absolution. When the soldiers of Henry II of England murdered Bishop Thomas Becket at Canterbury, the pope insisted that Henry be physically lashed as a part of his restoration to the church. So powerful did the church become that Pope Boniface VIII argued in a statement, "Unam Sanctum" (1302), that the relationship of the church and state was like that of the sun and the moon, whereby the state reflected the will of God in the life of the world. The assertion and exercise of this authority and power is called Caesaro-papism. This kind of authority and power was dangerous. The church lost sight of the potential for its own corruption, as in the case of simony—the sale and purchase of spiritual things for salvation. In both east and west the church expected to nurture the lives of the people as part of its responsibilities. The church expected the civil magistrate to support it through enforcing the tithe as well as the church's will in matters that made an impact on people's lives, often in areas where the temporal powers had a stake.

What was the relation of Christians to the world in which they lived during those years? This seems to have been a simple matter when the Christian community was small. As Paul wrote, it did not include many worldly wise, not many rich, not many powerful in its membership (see 1 Cor. 1:26). But because the church served the last, the least, and the lost of the society, it grew in its influence among all the people including the influential. When Emperor Constantine recognized the church, and after it finally was established as the religion of the empire, Christians assumed larger responsibilities. In this new situation, the church drew on Mosaic law, Roman law, and the teachings and example of Jesus Christ. It sanctified the cardinal virtues of prudence, temperance, fortitude, and justice. It added to these the theological virtues of faith, hope, and love. It blessed marriage by making it a sacrament, while not challenging the paternalist character of the institution. In the west, the economic system evolved into feudalism that mirrored the paternalist life in the economic sphere. It attempted to care for the poor and for slaves, but it did not decisively challenge the institution of slavery. In the earliest years, it appears that Christians were pacifists. But when soldiers, from the lowly recruits to the emperor, converted to Christianity, Christians had to deal with the questions: If to war, then when and how to war? Theologians such as Augustine accepted and refined a just-war theory for the Christian community.

Many Christians were deeply troubled by what they thought were unacceptable compromises they had to make in their faith and life. In an attempt to preserve a holiness they believed was required of Christians, some retreated into the wilderness as hermits. Simeon Stylites tried to live in adoration and intercession on a pole that grew higher and higher through the years until his death. Some retreated into monasteries or convents, taking vows of chastity, poverty, and obedience in order to escape contamination from the world. They offered for outsiders, who could not follow them in such austere commitment, continuous prayer for their salvation as well as their own. The Benedictine, Cisterian, Franciscan, and Dominican orders sprang up to satisfy the needs of such pilgrims. Francis of Assisi (1181–1226) vowed to live in poverty and to care for the poor, as did his followers. Clare, a noble lady of Assisi, organized a separate order ("Poor Clares") for women. These orders often contributed to the revitalization of the Christian mission, and they provided leadership in the church. As they grew in number, however, they also grew in wealth, influence, and power. They sometimes contributed to the evils from which those who entered the orders wished to escape. Moreover, by taking vows of celibacy and poverty, they also contributed to the belief that membership in these orders represented a higher form of Christian faith and life than available to married and working men or women.

The Road to Reformation

The world was excited at the end of the first millennium of the Christians era in 1000. A mystic known as Joachim of Fiori wrote reflections about the end time. He described three ages in the history of the world—the Father and the law in Hebrew Scriptures, the Son and the Christian Scriptures, and the Spirit that was dawning in his own time. Western Christians looked eastward and were inspired to join crusades to retake the Holy Land from Islam. So emperors, kings, noblemen, thousands of soldiers, and even children marched or sailed to Palestine in seven successive crusades. They were assured of their salvation as they sought this goal. They did succeed in recapturing Jerusalem and holding parts of the Middle East for over a century before finally being driven out by the Muslims. In the process, they sacked Christian Constantinople (on the fourth crusade), thus brutalizing themselves. In their zeal they also carried out persecutions of the Jews of Europe. Later, in 1453, the Turks took Constantinople and subsequently threatened to take Vienna, alarming all of Europe. At this time, the Russians who had become Orthodox Christians, declared Moscow a Third Rome, succeeding the city of Constantine, the Second Rome, as a vital center of the eastern church.

In the west, the Christian community experienced a period of widespread corruption in its life, practicing the seven deadly sins of pride, covetousness, lust, envy, gluttony, anger, and sloth. This was noted at the Council of Constance, where western Christians attempted to combat heresy and corruption in the church, beginning in 1414. They failed to do this. John Huss (c. 1372–1415), a Bohemian philosopher and reformer, was excommunicated and went to Constance for trial under the safe conduct of the emperor. The bishop of Constance imprisoned him despite the protests of the emperor. The council condemned him to die at the stake, a death he suffered courageously in 1415. Other devout Catholics, such as Englishman John Wycliffe, urged Christians to return to the Scriptures for a renewal of Christian faith and life, while Thomas á Kempis summoned believers to follow Jesus, through his reflections in his *Imitation of Christ* (c. 1418). After the Council of Constance, the call for reform grew even more insistent and intense, but also more difficult.

Martin Luther (1483–1546) became a catalyst for what is called the Protestant Reformation. Luther was a miner's son who became an Augustinian monk after his university training. He was born at a time when the church, under Pope Alexander VI of the Borgia family, was in a very low state. The pope, an astute politician and a patron of the arts, lived an immoral life. He and his immediate successors were involved in the sale of indulgences for the remission of sins on earth or in purgatory. The sale of these indulgences by professional pardoners, with some of the profit going for the building of St. Peter's Basilica in Rome, was a scandal to many Christians. Luther developed a deep anxiety about his own salvation and attempted to purify himself with good works, even volunteering to clean the latrines of the cloister to do penance for his real and imaginary sins. His relief came suddenly in his reflection on Paul's affirmation in his letter to the Romans that the "just shall live by faith" in the unmerited grace of God shown in the life, death, and resurrection of Jesus Christ (Rom. 1:16–17). Although Paul was known in the church, his central message of the unmerited graciousness of God had been neglected. Luther expressed his insights in the *Ninety-five Theses* that were then posted for debate. In 1520, he also printed three widely read tracts, printed on the new presses that had previously made the Bible and pamphlets available to the public. These tracts were *An Address to Christian Nobility,* which urged nobles to join in the reform of the church; the *Babylonian Captivity of the Church,* which attacked the church's sacramental system that seemed to deny the Christian of the true benefits of the gospel; and the *Christian Liberty,* in which Luther proclaimed the freedom of Christians from a works' righteousness, inviting them to freedom in God's promises to those who live by grace and by faith alone. Because of his teachings, Luther was summoned to the city of Worms for trial, which was presided over by Emperor Charles V. In his defense, Luther appealed to the Scriptures, under which authority both of his powerful adversaries, the emperor and the pope, professed to live. He held that unless he was shown by the Bible that he was wrong, "I shall not retract one iota, so Christ help me." Tradition also suggests that he exclaimed, "Here I stand, I cannot do otherwise." Luther, however, was declared a heretic and condemned. He was hunted by the forces of the emperor but was hidden and protected by German princes.

Under their patronage, he helped to shape the Lutheran Church through his sermons, commentaries, and other writings.

When Luther left the monastic life, he not only helped monks and nuns to marry, but married Katherine von Bora, with whom he lived and whom he loved with great affection. He sometimes called his beloved Katie "my rib," sometimes "my lord." She cared for their household and children. Through this marriage, Luther signaled rejection of celibacy as a higher form of Christian practice. He insisted on the priesthood of all believers in the church and the right of believers to receive the wine as well as the bread during the Lord's Supper. He also translated the Bible into German so the people might have access to the Word of Life in their own language, not simply in the Latin Vulgate. He was a brilliant and earthy conversationalist and controversialist. He angrily condemned German peasants for a rebellion, in which they were trying to gain justice for themselves and their families. He is also known negatively for expressions of anti-Semitism. Nevertheless, he is a monumental figure of the Reformation. The Roman Catholic Church, unable to ignore him and other reformers, called the Council of Trent (1545–1563), which carried out some reform while at the same time condemning Luther and his followers.

American Presbyterians inherited this past, which is often closer than today's believers realize.

2

The Birth of the
Reformed Tradition in Europe

"My heart I give you, Lord, eagerly and sincerely." John Calvin carried these words on his crest. The emblem presents a flaming heart held in a hand outstretched to God. Calvin (1509–1564) did not speak often of his conversion from Roman Catholicism to the French Protestant movement of the sixteenth century. It was sudden and deep, he wrote in a rare statement on the subject in his *Commentary on the Psalms* published in 1557. Although indebted to Martin Luther and other reformers, he made his own contributions to the Reformation, and his influence spread throughout Europe and the British Isles. American Presbyterians trace their own identity to him, one of the great formative figures of the Christians faith and life and western history.

As in the case of Luther, Calvin's conversion and spiritual pilgrimage took place during decisive changes in the human condition and situation. In the intellectual revolution known as the Renaissance, Europeans took a fresh look at the biblical, Greek, and Roman sources of western ideas and, in the process, changed how humans thought about themselves in relationship to the world. This intellectual stimulation led to scientific and technological breakthroughs that helped prove not only that the earth is almost round, but also that it, and the solar system, revolves around the sun. These developments quickened European exploration, exploitation, and colonization of the world. Medieval political and economic institutions gradually gave way to constitutional monarchies, representative governments, and early states of modern capitalism with the development of its middle class. All of these changes accelerated with a great change in communication. The development of the printing press greatly expanded literacy. This allowed a large number of people to read about and participate in these various revolutions. Presbyterian

seventeenth- and eighteenth-century ancestors were heirs of these up-
heavals. In turn, the Reformed made their own contributions to the emergence of the modern world. Here the focus is on John Calvin, the spread
of the Reformed movement in Europe, and the Reformed emphases in
worship, theology, and governance. Calvin and his followers also made
significant contributions to the development of education and to political
and economic life.

Calvin and the
Reformed Tradition

Reformation is a term used to describe religious movements, both Roman Catholic and Protestant, in the fifteenth and sixteenth centuries. Although Protestant is a term usually associated with Luther, it covers a
wide range of dissatisfaction with the Roman Catholic Church. It may be
interpreted in negative terms of protest, but it also points to positive al-
ternatives to Medieval Catholicism. Followers of Luther are usually
known by the name of the Wittenburg monk, turned reformer. Although
followers of Calvin were also called Calvinists, the Genevan's influence
produced variations on Calvinist themes. Those involved in this protest
became known as the Reformed. Another Protestant group, considered
more radical by Lutherans and the Reformed, were labeled Anabaptists
because of their felt need to be rebaptized. They were often more individ-
ualist and congregationalist in their church organization. Reformers were
genuinely concerned for the unity of Christ's body, but various pressures
and the emergence of the nation-state system complicated this quest.

Calvin, born in Noyon, France, originally intended to go into law. He
studied in leading French Universities, sharing the intellectual stimulation of the Renaissance. He published his first book on the Roman writer
Seneca, and in it attacked the political cynicism of Machiavelli of Florence
in the process. He also fell under the influence of French reformers, and
was converted at the age of twenty-three or -four. Because of the persecution of French Protestants, he fled to Switzerland where the climate was
more congenial and reform had already begun. Even before Calvin's arrival, Huldrych Zwingli (1484–1531) of Zurich and German-Swiss can-
tons, introduced reforms known for an emphasis on God's sovereignty
and its rather austere worship and life. Zwingli placed on emphasis on the
sermon and two Sacraments: Baptism and the Lord's Supper. He considered the latter a memorial in which Christ was present by the power of
the Holy Spirit. Zwingli's reform was known also for a stern morality. A
few years after Zwingli's death, Calvin published the first edition of the

Institutes of the Christian Religion (1536), his most famous statement of the Reformed faith. He dedicated it to the King of France and summoned France to reform. At the same time, he was persuaded by William Farel, somewhat against his judgment, that he should remain in Geneva to labor for the church. Because of what he felt to be unwarranted interference in ecclesiastical matters, Calvin left Geneva for Strasburg, to return only when invited back by the city as its pastor.

In Geneva, Calvin gave shape to the city's religious life. He focused on the worship of God throughout the community, developing a form of adoration involving the full participation of the people. Public psalm singing brought tears to the eyes of Genevans. Calvin also devoted prodigious energy and much time to preaching, commenting on the Scriptures, and teaching theology. He continued to revise and expand the *Institutes,* the last edition of which appeared in 1558. He also reorganized the governance of the church under a representative system of pastors and laity, continuing to preserve a proper relation with the civil magistrates of the city. Contrary to commonly held views of the reformer's power and authority, these magistrates did not always approve of what Calvin wanted to do. However, he did have a profound impact on the social, political, and economic life of the city. Calvin married Idelette de Bure, a widow with an Anabaptist background. They had one son, who died in infancy. They loved each other deeply throughout their brief marriage, marred by the ill health of both of them. After her early death, Calvin wrote that she was the "best companion of my life," a great help to his work.

Scottish reformer, John Knox, who fled his country to live in Geneva for a time, called the city "the most perfect school of Christ that ever was in the earth since the days of the apostles." That may have been an exaggeration. Calvin himself was irritable and sometimes lost his temper, often fighting with the city fathers. Moreover, he supplied both Roman Catholics and Protestant authorities with evidence of heresy against Michael Servetus, who was burned at the stake in Geneva in 1553 for denying the doctrine of the Trinity. Catholics and Lutherans would have burned the heretic had he fallen into their hands. Calvin pleaded for Servetus to be hung rather than burned. This plea, however, does not excuse Calvin nor take away this stain from his record. Nevertheless, the Geneva reformer influenced all Europe through his published writings and his enormous correspondence, in which he dispensed advice and comfort. In these writings he demonstrated his pastoral heart. He once wrote a mourning friend after a death in the family that nowhere in the "school of Christ" are Christians required to put off humanity. Human beings are not stone. However, having "shed those tears," which are caused by "nature and fatherly affection," he advised, "we should not give way to senseless wailing." Christians should set some bounds to sadness and live in hope. Exiles who visited Geneva carried his ideas throughout Europe. In this way Calvin strengthened the movements in France, Germany, Holland, Eastern Europe, and the British Isles.

The Genevan reformer influenced the French Protestants, who were also known as *Huguenots*. The derivation of the word *Huguenot* is uncertain, perhaps a corruption of the word meaning confederate. It may refer to the ghost of a saintly King Hugo, who allegedly walked abroad at night, since Huguenots had to meet at night to avoid persecution. Beginning as a congregational movement, Gallican Protestantism soon grew, enjoying the protection of Marguerite of Angouleme (1492–1549), Queen of Navarre, who had Reformed sympathies. Marguerite was one of the notable women who supported the Reformation and who wrote plays and poems in order to express her religious commitments. In one of her poems, which appeared in Roland Bainton's *Women in the Reformation*, she discusses justification by faith alone.

> To you I testify
> That God does justify
> Through Christ, the man who sins,
> But if he does not believe
> And by faith receive
> He shall have no peace
> From worry no surcease.
> God will then relieve,
> If faith will not believe
> Through Christ, the gentle Lord.

Huguenots were able to organize a synodical form of government on a national scale, thus giving strength to the constituents. The church developed its own form of worship and the Gallican Confession (1559), which gave expression to Reformed faith and life in France. The spread of the movement alarmed Roman Catholics, who butchered thousands of Protestants in the shocking massacre of St. Bartholomew's Day in 1572. Protestants recalled this event for centuries. Henry of Navarre, a Reformed heir to the throne, turned Catholic—a kingdom, he is supposed to have said, is worth a mass. But he also issued the Edict of Nantes in 1598, granting toleration to the Calvinists. This act was a milestone on the way to religious freedom, although the Huguenots continued to be persecuted under subsequent Catholic monarchs.

After Zwingli, Johann Heinrich Bullinger (1504–1575) strengthened the Reformed movement in the German-speaking areas of Switzerland and Europe. Bullinger also had widespread influence all over the continent because of his scholarship and because of the *First* and *Second Helvetic Confessions* with their emphasis on covenant theology. Under King Frederick III, Calvinism spread in the Rhineland. The king encouraged Calvinist scholars Zacharias Ursinus (d. 1583) and Kaspar Olevianus (d. 1587). These theologians composed the *Heidelberg Cathechism* (1563), based on the letter of Paul to the church at Rome. This catechism was widely used, especially among the Reformed in the Netherlands. When this area came under his control by inheritance, Catholic King Philip II of Spain set out to restore Roman Catholicism in northern Europe. He was especially concerned about the Netherlands because of its move toward Protestantism and its flourishing economic life under William the Silent, Prince of Orange. The Dutch "beggars," as they were called by Philip, engaged in a bloody conflict to throw off the Spanish yoke. William finally won independence. Dutch Protestants developed their own form of Reformed worship, a *Belgic Confession* (1566), and a synodical form of governance. Perhaps because of their experience with persecution, as well as a sense that intolerance was bad for business, the Dutch developed a more tolerant, multicultural trading nation. Reformed influences also spread eastward into Bohemia, Poland, and Hungary, and especially into Transylvania, where reformers developed their own ethnic forms of worship, using Bullinger's *Second Helvetic Confession* (1566). They organized a form of government that included episcopal leadership. As already indicated, the continental Reformed movement shaped Protestantism in the British Isles, further expanding the multiethnic character of Calvin's influence.

Worship, Theology, and Governance in Geneva

Calvin and those in the Reformed tradition shared many convictions with Roman Catholics, Lutherans, Anabaptists, and other Protestants. However, if Luther was the great theologian of justification by grace and faith alone, Calvin and his followers focused on the glory of God. "Now the great thing is this," Calvin wrote in the *Institutes*:

> We are consecrated and dedicated to God in order that we may thereafter think, speak, meditate, and do nothing except to his glory. . . . We are God's: let us therefore live for him and die for him. We are God's: let his wisdom and will therefore rule all our actions. We

are God's: let all the parts of our life accordingly strive toward him
as our only lawful goal. O, how much has that man profiteth who,
having been taught that he is not his own, has taken away dominion
and rule from his own reason that he may yield it to God!

This biblical vision of a God who grasped and controlled all life shaped
Reformed worship, theology, governance, and the Christian life.

Worship, according to the Reformed tradition is the Christian's chief
service to God. Worship is inspired and supported by the Holy Spirit. It
includes the preaching and the hearing of the Word and the sacramental
life initiated by Jesus Christ in his own ministry. One of the earliest things
Calvin did in Geneva was to lay out his views of worship—biblically oriented, marked by theological integrity, intelligibility, and simplicity. It
was for the edification of the whole Christian community. Calvin provided a form of worship that included written as well as spontaneous
prayers. His order began with Psalm 124:8: "Our help is in the name of
the LORD, who made heaven and earth." The first part of the service focused on the preaching of the Word. Such preaching was invigorated by
the accessibility of the Bible in print and in the vernacular, not simply in
the Latin of the Vulgate. The Reformed, as did the Lutherans, did away
with the medieval sacramental system, retaining only Baptism through
sprinkling (including infants of believing parents) and the Lord's Supper.
Calvin taught that Christ was present spiritually and not physically
through "transubstantiation," a medieval scholastic term. Calvin wanted
the Lord's Supper to be celebrated every Sunday. The civil authorities dis-
sented. But Calvin did manage to schedule services in Genevan churches
so that the sacrament was observed somewhere in the city on every Lord's
Day. The Reformed became known as Psalm singers. Psalms were biblical and therefore orthodox. Calvin was not, however, opposed to what
became known as hymns of human composition. Louis Bourgeois was in
charge of music in the city. Calvin once rescued him after the musician
was thrown in jail by the magistrate for tune-tampering with familiar
hymns. Calvin reassured the authorities that Bourgeois was simply trying
to improve congregational singing by the use of tunes that were derisively
called Geneva "jigs."

Calvin developed forms not only for Sunday worship, but for Baptism,
marriage, and the visitation of the sick, allowing for written as well as free
prayer. According to the rite of 1542, morning worship consisted of two
parts: the Liturgy of the Word and the Liturgy of the Upper Room.

The Liturgy of the Word

Scripture Sentence Psalm 124:8
Confession of Sins

Prayer for Pardon
Metrical Psalm
Collect for Illumination
Lection
Sermon

The Liturgy of the Upper Room
Collection of alms
Intercessions
Lord's Prayer in long paraphrase
Preparation of Elements sung with Apostles' Creed
Words of Institution
Exhortation
Consecration Prayer
Fraction
Delivery
Communion, with Psalm or Scripture
Post-communion Collect
Aaronic Blessing

Reformed theology, then, was confessional and concerned about affirming what is believed about God and our human nature and destiny. Although his most extensive writings are biblical commentaries, Calvin himself is still known primarily as a theologian because of his *Institutes*, which he revised throughout his lifetime. As his theology developed, Calvin organized his material more and more around the Apostles' Creed, which was recited in worship. The Reformed, following Calvin, based their theology on scripture. They also accepted the ancient creeds of the church. The Reformed held that we cannot know God in the divine perfection, but in the way in which God relates as Creator and Redeemer, and by the work of the Holy Spirit testifying in the heart. The Reformed were Trinitarians who expressed the mystery of God's relations in terms of the ancient creeds. As Creator, God is powerful and purposeful, calling into being created order, creating human beings in God's own image, making human stewards of the creation. The Reformed affirmed the goodness of creation, although still "groaning," as Paul wrote, for completion (Rom. 8:22). As Redeemer, God delivers humans from sinfulness and alienation from the divine purposes in an age of anxiety. Human beings fall short of God's intentions in all that they do in this life. Even what from a human perspective appears good is spoiled by human pride. Calvin analyzed this as a tendency toward idolatry and self-worship. In the later editions of the *Institutes*,

Calvin gave much attention to the Roman Catholic veneration of relics, and maintained that the scholastic difference between veneration and worship was, more often than not, lost on the ordinary sinner looking for a way out of the abyss of life. The result of this alienation is the sin and death that permeates the whole created order and thwarts God's will.

Humans know God the Redeemer through Jesus Christ, encountered through the Scriptures. Through Christ, God manifests unmerited love. In his commentaries, Calvin deals with all aspects of Christ's salvific life: as a sacrificial lamb, a shepherd giving life for the sheep, an offering of atonement by a priest, a ransom of a slave, a payment of a debt, a vicarious sacrifice for a legal penalty, and victory over the powers of evil. Calvin emphasized Christ's priestly work (Heb. 9:14, 25–26), combined with the legal language of the Scriptures (Gal. 3:13). As did Luther, the Reformed stressed God's grace in the restoration of our relationship with the divine. In this connection, Calvin explored the problem of predestination, an issue he felt he had to face because of the ancient problem of freedom and determinism. He found this concern for election expressed in the Scriptures. Calvin's legal mind pressed him to reflect on this matter in relation to God's omnipotence and omniscience. He was very uncomfortable about doing so because it led him to affirm a double election, to salvation, or to death and separation from God. Calvin treated his discussion of this matter when writing about God's free grace in Jesus Christ. He considered it a comforting doctrine for the believer, but he warned against endless speculation over this matter.

This problem of election surfaced at the Synod of Dort in the Netherlands, 1618–1619, an ecumenical conference of Protestants who gathered to respond to Jacobus Arminius, who stressed human freedom in the matter of our response to God. The Synod stressed total depravity, unconditional election, limited atonement, irresistible grace, and the perseverance of the saints in order to preserve the doctrine of salvation by grace alone and not by works. It is largely because of this Synod that the Reformed became known as predestinarians. This problem continued to cause tension among Presbyterians. Verses in a hymn found in the French Psalter of 1545, often ascribed to Calvin, present another side of the Reformed faith and life at this point.

> I greet Thee, who my sure Redeemer art,
> My only trust and Savior of my heart,
> Who pain didst undergo for my poor sake;
> I pray Thee from our hearts all cares to take.

Thou hast the pure and perfect gentleness,
No harshness hast Thou and no bitterness;
O grant to us the grace to find in Thee,
That we may dwell in perfect unity.

Our hope is in no other save in Thee;
Our faith is built upon Thy promise free;
Lord, give us peace, and make us calm and sure,
That in Thy strength we evermore endure.

The *Heidelberg Cathechism* also expresses and summarizes the Reformed view of God's grace. This catechetical question and answer stresses the Reformed view of hope.

Q. What is your only comfort, in life and in death?
A. That I belong—body and soul, in life and in death—not to myself but to my faithful Savior, Jesus Christ, who at the cost of his own blood has fully paid for all my sins and has completely freed me from the dominion of the devil; that he protects me so well that without the will of my Father in heaven not a hair can fall from my head; indeed, that everything must fit his purpose for my salvation. Therefore, by his Holy Spirit, he also assures me of eternal life, and makes me wholeheartedly willing and ready from now on to live for him.

God in Christ has overcome evil. Sin and death will not triumph. God makes "all things new" and will bring about a "new heaven and a new earth." Furthermore, God gives the Holy Spirit who witnesses here and now to God the Creator and Redeemer. The Spirit draws believers into community with one another and inspires Christians to discipleship in response to God's love.

Structures of Grace:
The Church and Educational,
Political, and Economic Life

In the Reformed view of the church, God calls the Christian community into being through the work of Christ and the Holy Spirit. The church is a community of faith and life that is called to share Christ's story with the world. As such, Christians belong to a communion of saints, not a hierarchical order in heaven but a community of the dead and the living, the number of which is known only to God. This view led to a perception of the church both as an invisible body, known only to God, and as the visible church in the world, as a primary structure of grace. The Reformed maintained that governance in the Christian family is an expression of Christian belief. Calvin and his followers returned to the Scriptures to explore ideas for the structuring of the church. Calvin expressed these ideas in the *Institutes* and his *Ecclesiastical Ordinances* (1541). Other Reformed leaders followed Calvin and expressed their views in other confessions, as well as statements about church government.

Jesus Christ is the only head of the church. The Reformed believed that in the Roman Catholic Church the pope usurped Christ's authority and power and was not a reliable representative of it. The Reformed believed in the priesthood, the prophethood, and the kingship of all believers. They also believed that apostolic succession involved the consecration of the Spirit, and that it is found where the Word is truly preached and the sacraments of Baptism and the Lord's Supper are properly administered, not in the presence of the bishop. Most of the Reformed rejected the monarchical and the hierarchical church government and moved toward the conciliar model, which emphasized the parity of the clergy and lay participation in church governance. Thus they expressed their disdain for the papal bureaucracy with its popes, cardinals, bishops, archbishops, arch-this and arch-that—its many ecclesiastical underlings. Calvin found only four types of church officers in the Bible: *pastors* and *teachers,* who were responsible for worship and education; *elders,* who were responsible for discipline; and *deacons,* who were responsible for the care of the poor, indigent, and the sick in congregations.

The Genevan church was run by a consistory responsible for encouraging Christian discipleship. In larger geographical areas such as France, the Netherlands, and other parts of Europe, the Reformed developed a system of graduated church bodies, beginning with the congregation, then the consistory or presbytery, and all embraced in a synod. These structures were collegial in form and were concerned for decency and order and due process in dealing with the health of the whole Christian family. The overall purpose of the governance was to assist in the sanctification of the believer through the nurturing of forgiveness, reconciliation, and discipline. Some Reformed churches, for example, in Geneva, in the Netherlands, in the British Isles, were allied with the civil authorities and depended on that authority for financial support and the implementation of discipline in various ways. However, the Reformed church leaders attempted to keep the states from interference in the ecclesiastical realm.

While the Reformed tradition fragmented into ethnic churches as the Reformation spread, Calvin and his followers expressed concern about the unity of the church across state boundaries. Whereas affirming the oneness of the Christian family made possible by the Holy Spirit, the Reformed also attempted to express a visible unity not only among themselves but also by trying to build bridges across Protestant boundaries. Theodore Beza, Calvin's successor in Geneva, prepared the *Harmony of Confessions* (1581), a book of fifteen Protestant catechisms and confessional statements, to express the theological unity they had in Christ. Hugo Grotius, an Arminian in the Netherlands, promoted international law that should govern the relations between the emerging states.

The Reformed stressed literacy and education, made all the more important because of the availability of the Bible and the expanding learning of those years. Calvin was trained in the university and so drank deeply from the well of medieval learning and the Renaissance. The Reformed considered the teacher among the church offices sanctioned in the Scripture. All believers, the Reformed held, should have access to the Scriptures, the rule of faith and life, and learning, and were called to serve God with all the gifts of divine grace. Therefore, Calvin and his followers stressed universal education. In Geneva, for example, the *Ecclesiastical Ordinances* ruled that the "youth should be faithfully instructed." This included poor youth and women, who were to receive elementary education. This was a small but important step in the advancement of women's lives. Calvin participated in this process. He even complained once to the City Council about a student who was shooting peas at one of the instructors. The only major construction that took place in Geneva during Calvin's life, except for roads and fortifications, was the college. In this way the Reformed stimulated the life of the mind.

The Reformed made a contribution in the political structures primarily through the participation of people in representative constitutional governments. Civil magistracy is a gift of God to encourage just and compassionate human behavior and to discourage and restrain evil. The Reformed knew from their studies of the Greek and Roman classics, and through their own experiences, various forms of government and their dangers—monarchy and tyranny (the rule of one), aristocracy and oligarchy (the rule of the few), democracy and mobocracy (the rule of the mob). Just as they were moved toward a participatory and representative system of government in ecclesiastical matters, so they moved in this direction in the political sphere. While not rejecting monarchy altogether, they advocated a combination of democracy with an aristocracy of merit as the best form of government. This form would provide the proper checks and balances to control our tendency to draw to our own interests and to promote civic responsibility. With regard to the right of revolution, the Reformed were cautious. Yet Calvin suggested that the lower magistrate might overthrow a tyrant who ruled contrary to God's will. After the massacre of St. Bartholomew's Day, Huguenots developed a theory of tyranicide while remaining sympathetic to monarchy. The Revocation of the Edict of Nantes in 1685 by Louis XIV of France did nothing to enhance the French monarchy in the eyes of the Huguenots, many of whom fled their country for Britain or the American colonies. As indicated with regard to the church, Christians were called to be yeast, not only nurturing responsible life within the church but practicing forgiveness and reconciliation so essential to the body politic as well as the body of Christ.

Calvinists also made a contribution to economic life as Feudalism gave way to double-column bookkeeping and modern capitalism. The Reformed did not hold that there was an autonomous sphere of economic laws apart from God's laws that require justice and compassion. God calls Christians to responsible economic life, as well as to salvation, to seek the public good and not private interest. Calvinists did away with medieval monastic institutions and denied that monastic life was a higher order of Christian life. They forbade mendicant orders, which claimed that such a life was a higher order of Christian obedience. Calvinists believed that all people should work using the gifts God gives to each person. Moreover, Calvinists did not place people in fixed orders. They allowed movement in occupations, as peoples' interests and skills developed. Calvin did away with the medieval prohibition against interest and allowed investors to earn a fair return on the lending of money. He also held that Christians should live disciplined and simple lives. Because of this, he helped foster capitalism and savings for investment. Calvin and later Reformed leaders did *not* teach that the accumulation of wealth was a sign of God's election. To the contrary, Calvin warned against fraud, and also warned that a rich person might not get through the "needle's eye" (Matt. 19:24). Riches may blind the wealthy so that they cannot see conditions of others whose lives may depend on them. Calvin maintained that the magistrate had a responsibility to find employment for Genevans and to care for the indigent.

The Reformed tradition with its various emphases spread throughout the continent. This was the primary mission field of the early Reformers. The Reformed influence also spread to the British Isles—to England, Scotland, and Northern Ireland—and then to America. Calvin, it should be noted, supported a colonization project of the Huguenots to Brazil in 1557 and also a settlement in Florida (1562). The latter was destroyed when the Spanish put the Huguenots to death. Calvinism spread, with its emphasis on worship, on theology, on representative government in ecclesiastical as well as political structures. The Reformed carried with them an important affirmation of Christian Reformed faith and life: *Ecclesia reformata, semper reformanda,* the church reformed, always being reformed under the Word of God. This affirmation helped them further some of the most formative and dynamic aspects of modern life.

3

The British Isles: Scotland, England, and Ireland

"God is English," Bishop John Aylmer declared in 1559. The Bishop figured it this way. The Englishman John Wycliffe begot Huss. Huss begot Luther. Luther begot the truth about the Gospel. So Christ was pleased to be born again of an Englishman among the English. Of course, Christian faith and life had been born in the British Isles as early as A.D. 200. Later, Patrick, who was from west England, became the instrument for the conversion of Ireland in the fifth century. His successor, Columba, made his way to Iona on the coast of Scotland and converted many of the Scots. The missionary, Augustine, not to be confused with the patristic theologian, brought all England under the sign of the cross. By the sixteenth century, the British expressed concern for reform and came under the influence of Luther. Aylmer might have named other English reformers such as William Tyndale, whose translations of the New Testament into English, according to the bishop, were one means of Christ's rebirth in the British Isles.

The Reformation in the British Isles in the sixteenth and seventeenth centuries involved a spiritual awakening that turned out to be largely Reformed in its sympathies. It also involved political struggles to unify England, Scotland, and Ireland under one crown, under William and Mary as a constitutional monarchy. Henry VIII (1491–1547) of England declared himself the head of Christ's church when in his pursuit of a male heir, the pope refused to annul King Henry's marriage with Catherine of Aragon. Henry tried to preserve Roman Catholicism as "defender of the faith," countering the influences of Luther with his own writings. On his death, Calvin's influence came to the fore under the boy King Edward VI and his guardian, Thomas Cranmer (1489–1556), as may be seen in aspects of the *Book of Common Worship* (1549), a great legacy of those years. Cranmer's Calvinist touch may be seen in the great prayer of confession:

> Almighty and merciful God, We have erred and strayed from Thy
> ways like lost sheep. We have followed too much the devices and de-
> sires of our own hearts. We have offended against Thy holy laws. We
> have left undone those things we ought to have done; and we have
> done those things which we ought not to have done; and there is no
> health in us. But Thou, O Lord, have mercy upon us, miserable of-
> fenders. Spare Thou those, O God, who confess their faults. Restore
> Thou those who are penitent according to Thy promises declared
> unto mankind in Christ Jesus our Lord. And grant, O most merciful
> Father, for His sake, that we may hereafter live a godly, righteous,
> and sober life to the glory of Thy holy name. Amen.

Mary Tudor restored Catholicism, persecuting Protestants, burning Cranmer at the stake, and driving dissenters out. They found refuge in places such as Geneva. After Mary's death, Elizabeth I (1558–1603), a shrewed political leader, became a Protestant while trying to keep some of the trappings of Rome. She referred to herself as the governor, rather than the head, of Christ's church. Under the Act of Supremacy and the Act of Uniformity (1559), she tried to force a religious unity on her subjects by making them accept a creedal statement, the *Thirty-nine Articles* of the Church of England (1553, 1571), and worship according to the *Book of Common Prayer*. England was Reformed in theology. Nonconformists such as Presbyterians and Congregationalists, known also as Puritans, and more radical religious groups, lost political and economic privileges to adherents of the established church. The history of Protestantism involved a conflict in Scotland, England, and Ireland, over worship, theology, and especially the form of the government of Christ's church. After the Tudors, the battles continued under Stuart monarchs until William and Mary came from the Netherlands to the throne in 1688. These conflicts reverberated in the American colonies.

Reform in Scotland

In the beginning, Presbyterian faith and life flourished in Scotland rather than in England as the Scots resisted English influence over their lives. In the British Isles the Scots were the first to feel Luther's impact. Patrick Hamilton, after studying in France, brought Luther's teachings back to Scotland. For this he was burned at the stake. His martyrdom in 1528 lit fires for reform, despite attempts of the Catholics to strengthen ties with Rome and to form an alliance with France. Because of French power in Scotland, the English found it in their interest to encourage Reformation, which flowed from Geneva and other Calvinist centers. So Scotland was Reformed before John Knox (ca. 1514–1571), a Roman Catholic in background, became its leading figure. He then proceeded to cut the influence of the papacy "at its roots."

Knox was educated at Glasgow and became involved in the conflict of the Scots with the French. The French captured and sent him to row in a galley for nineteen months. This punishment did nothing good for his disposition. He then spent part of his ministry in England before joining the Marian exiles in Geneva. While in Geneva, learning from Calvin, he participated in the translation of the *Geneva Bible* (1560) and also wrote *The First Blast of the Trumpet against The Monstrous Regiment of Women* (1558). In this exclamation, he attacked Roman Catholic Mary Tudor of England and Mary of Guise, Queen of Scotland. Knox aimed primarily at their Catholicism. But he also asserted that women rulers represented an unnatural order of things. Calvin thought his *Blast* intemperate. Elizabeth, who came to the throne in 1558, did too, and was not happy with the man who became Scotland's most celebrated minister. He returned to Scotland in 1559 in time to give thanks in St. Giles Cathedral for the withdrawal of French and English forces from his homeland.

The Scottish Parliament then proceeded to abolish Roman Catholicism and establish a Presbyterian Church from the top down. Parliament adopted Knox's *The Forme of Prayers* (1560), which showed his indebtedness to Calvin. He also placed an emphasis on the Bible, which he believed prescribed the elements of Christian worship. His opposition to the "idolatrous" Mass led him to emphasize the Old Testament and to a pronounced literalness. The Scots became Psalm singers who delighted in the gifts of William Kethe. When in Geneva, Kethe adapted Psalm 100 for an "Anglo-Genevan Psalter":

> All people that on earth do dwell,
> Sing to the Lord with cheerful voice;
> Him serve with mirth, His praise forth tell,
> Come ye before Him and rejoice.

In the *Scots Confession* (1560), Knox embraced the doctrinal traditions of the early church. He placed an emphasis on the Reformation view of the faith, justification and sanctification, Scripture and its authority, Christ's offices as prophet, priest, and king, the church and sacraments, and the civil authority. Knox did not highlight predestination. He commended other Reformed confessions to Christians.

In *The First Book of Discipline* (1560), Knox defended Presbyterian order as biblical. The Parliament imposed this form with graduated governing bodies under a General Assembly on Scotland. Knox did not reject, absolutely, a place for bishops in the church. He even allowed for the temporary use of the office of superintendent to oversee the church's life. He also expected the cooperation of the civil as well as the ecclesiastical powers in fostering true religion, but did not approve of the state interfering with the authority of the church. When Mary Stuart returned from France to rule Scotland, Knox entered into hostile combat with her about her political powers. He often made her weep in anger. Eventually, personal scandal forced her into exile. Knox made provision for universal education in Scotland. He insisted that the government deal with the needs of the indigent and poor, since he felt that people in such condition should not be the subject of charity only. He even allowed some possibility of revolt against political tyranny.

Knox's successor, Andrew Melville (1545–1622), emerged to strengthen the Presbyterian movement in Scotland. He opposed episcopacy in every form, and in his *Discipline* he declared that in the Bible "bishops," "pastors," and "ministers" were equivalent terms. Ministers must be elected by the people. He regularized the meetings of church assemblies—local, provincial, and national. He was also concerned for churches in "all and diverse nations," illustrating his ecumenical interest. Although he expected the state to assist the church in various ways, he opposed the assumption of the spiritual sword by James VI when he moved from Scotland to the throne in England. Melville referred to James as "God's silly vassal" and reminded him that "King James is the subject of King Jesus. . . . You are not the head of the Church." Needless to say, James, who became James I of England, was suspicious of such plain speaking Presbyterians. Hamilton, Knox, Melville, and others left their mark on the Presbyterian Church in Scotland. This church in turn had considerable influence on developments in England, Ireland, and America.

Reform in England

While Scotland continued its Reformation, Elizabeth carried on her own in England, identifying with the Protestant cause. She attempted, as did her father, to keep as much tradition as possible to satisfy her Roman Catholic subjects. This did not satisfy those who came to be known as

Puritans, some of whom wanted radical reform "without tarrying." The more moderate Puritans formed themselves into at least two major parties, the Presbyterians and the Congregationalists. These Protestants disagreed over the biblical form of church government. The parties sometimes cooperated in pushing for a Presbyterian form of government for the Church of England, as in an Admonition to Parliament (1572). Elizabeth resisted these moves against episcopacy. Many ministers refused to conform and were removed from their pulpits and from professorships, as was Thomas Cartwright (c. 1535–1603), a leader of the Presbyterian party. Some ministers went to prison. Shortly after this, Elizabeth executed Mary Stuart for conspiracy against her reign. Philip II (1529–1598) of Spain, who had seen Mary as one means of reestablishing Catholicism in England, mounted the Spanish Armada to accomplish this purpose. As the Spanish fleet moved northward in 1588, it first was attacked by Elizabeth's fleet and then was almost destroyed by what Protestants took to be a providential storm. Some Spanish survivors sailed around Britain to Ireland and then back to Spain. The defeat removed the Spanish threat and encouraged England in its exploration and colonization of what became English America, giving birth to the British Empire. Although Elizabeth had presided effectively over the blossoming of Shakespearean culture, she was not able to settle the religious conflict.

After her death in 1603, Elizabeth was succeeded by James VI of Scotland, who became James I of England. Although a Calvinist in theology, he did not like Presbyterians. Because of his own experiences, he complained of a "Scottish Presbytery which as well agreeth with a monarchy as God with the devil." Presbyterians allowed any "Tom and Will and Dick" to censure a king. He did not like Congregationalists either. Their church polity was even more democratic than the Presbyterian, and they were more liberal politically. James worried: "No Bishop, no King." He agreed to the Puritan proposal to bring forth a new version of the Bible. He did this in part to get rid of the *Geneva Bible,* which carried marginal notes that he thought subversive of the monarchy. An ecumenical group of scholars brought forth the *King James Version* (1611), which became the authorized Bible of the country. This Bible shaped the language as well as the religious consciousness of English-speaking people for centuries. In this period, some Congregationalists, as well as some Presbyterians, began to leave England for New England with a desire to be a "City on a Hill," to show what old England's reformation should be. In the New World, Roger Williams (1603–1683), a defender of religious liberty, engaged in a sharp debate with John Cotton (1584–1652), another Reformed clergyman, about this matter in the 1640s and 1650s.

When in 1625 Charles I came to the throne with his Catholic wife, a bloody Civil War broke out, engulfing Scotland and Ireland as well as England. Presbyterians and Congregationalists, who sometimes fought among themselves, took up arms against Charles and his royalist forces. The Scots revolted. When Charles attempted to impose English worship in Scotland, it caused a riot in St. Gile's Church in Edinburgh. A demonstrative Janet Geddes is reported to have thrown a stool at a clergyman's head when the latter celebrated what Geddes took to be the Mass. Charles's actions led to a "National Covenant" (1638) made by nobles, gentry, clergy, and peasants who pledged to defend the Church of Scotland. Charles finally reached an agreement with the Scots, but he then angered the Congregationalists and others by attempting to arrest leaders of Parliament after he had called it into session in 1640. The Scots and the English entered into a "Solemn League and Covenant" (1643) against the king. With regard to religious matters, Parliament called the Westminster Assembly while Charles was still king to reach an ecumenical settlement for the British Isles. This Assembly met in Westminster Abbey between 1643 and 1648, during the Civil War. One hundred and twenty-one commissioners from various religious backgrounds, assisted by some very capable and influential Scottish Presbyterians, met to reform the Church of England, making it "more agreeable to the Word of God."

The commissioners produced several major documents dealing with worship, theology, and discipline, all extremely important for Presbyterians, who played decisive roles in the meetings. These participants wrote *The Directory for Public Worship* (1644) to replace the *Book of Common Prayer*. The dissenters thoroughly disliked the latter because of its association with the Act of Supremacy and the Act of Uniformity. Instead of a book of prescribed elements for worship and prayer, the *Directory* offered definitions and directions that would preserve all the components of true devotion but allow maximum freedom in the worship of Almighty God. Those who wrote the *Directory* provided a definition of worship, which included a number of elements—the reading of the Bible, public prayer, preaching, and Baptism and the Lord's Supper. With regard to singing, the House of Commons, on the advice of the Assembly, and in the interest of uniformity between England and Scotland, authorized the use of a version of the *Psalms* by Francis Rous. This psalm book was revised by the General Assembly of Scotland and brought out in 1650. It was to be sung with a few memorized tunes laid out by a precentor. Psalm 23 became a favorite:

> The Lord's my Shepherd, I'll not want;
> He makes me down to lie

In pastures green; He leadeth me
The quiet waters by.

Goodness and mercy all my life
Shall surely follow me;
And in God's house forevermore
My dwelling place shall be.

Presbyterians became almost exclusively Psalm singers, as in Geneva. This led to contention among them as Presbyterian appreciation of church music expanded.

Commissioners also composed the *Westminster Confession of Faith* (1647) and the *Westminster Larger* and *Shorter Catechisms* to replace the *Thirty-nine Articles* of the Church of England. The confession and catechisms were scholastic, more abstract, expressions of Protestantism than earlier such statements. The writers used insights from the original Reformers such as Calvin, but laid out in a more logical, systematic, and complete way. The *Westminster Confession* begins with a Reformation affirmation about the sources of our knowledge of God. These include the "light of nature, and the works of creation and providence." It emphasized that the primary source for the Christian of the knowledge of God's saving acts is the Scripture. The Bible teaches about God's intention for the creation and for human redemption through Jesus Christ. The Scripture becomes God's Word as the Spirit, according to the *Confession,* witnesses "by and with" the Word in the believer's heart. The commissioners, as good Calvinists, also emphasized God's lordship over all life. Whereas confessing that God is ultimately "incomprehensible" the writers nevertheless defined God in the *Shorter Catechism* in the trinitarian terms of the early church, and as "a Spirit, infinite, eternal, and unchangeable, in his being, wisdom, power, holiness, justice, goodness, and truth." The *Confession* gave prominence to the doctrine of election, predestination, and foreordination, but dealt with God's sovereignty and human freedom in such a way that it did not attempt to resolve the tension of this theological problem. The commissioners, following an emphasis of the Congregationalists, also stressed the covenant of work and the covenant of grace. In this way they were able to develop their concerns for the Christians faith, the end of which is not simply forgiveness, but faithful discipleship. They emphasized the transformation of Christian life into a witness to the Kingdom of God.

This comes out in the treatment by the *Larger* and *Shorter Catechisms* of the Ten Commandments and what is required and what is forbidden in them in the acknowledgment of God and of human behavior. In dealing with false witness, for example, the *Larger Catechism* forbids Christians to keep "an undue silence in a just cause." The Westminster Assembly defined the civil magistrate in a positive way, as a gift from God, to encourage the good and to restrain evil. Christians may also, according to the commissioners, engage in war on "just and necessary occasions." While allowing magistrates to call meetings of church councils, the *Confession* also asserts that "God alone is the Lord of Conscience" in matters contrary to God's will. The confession and catechisms also deal with the reconciliation that flows from Baptism and the Lord's Supper to the Christian and the whole Christian family. The purpose of these confessional documents was to underscore the focus of the Christian faith and life. This good was most succinctly put in the first question and answer to the *Shorter Catechism*:

> Q. What is the chief end of man [and woman]?
> A. Man's [and woman's] chief end is to glorify God, and to enjoy him forever.

The commissioners had the most difficulty and expressed their differences in the area of ecclesiastical governance. In *The Form of Presbyterial Church Government* (1644), they described the nature and function of pastors and teachers. The Westminster Assembly of Divines referred to church governors in ambiguous terms because of tension among the Assembly members over the biblical form of church government. This debate was related to the conflict over the authority, power, and form of civil government that was taking place in the political sphere in the conflict with the Royalists. Here the Assembly failed the Presbyterians who were often in control of the Parliament. With regard to the outcome of the Westminster Assembly, the Scots adopted the documents without setting aside the previous positions taken by Presbyterians in Scotland. The Congregationalists were less enthusiastic.

Congregationalist Oliver Cromwell (1599–1658) controlled the army. He was angered with the English Presbyterians, as well as the Scots, for opposing the beheading of Charles I who was declared a tyrant. Moreover, he considered some Presbyterians as intolerant, agreeing with John Milton, his Latin secretary, that "New presbyter is but old priest writ large." Samuel Butler ridiculed Presbyterians in another way:

> They prove their doctrine orthodox
> By apostolic blows and knocks.

Cromwell made war on the Scots when they opposed developments in England, and even dispensed with the Presbyterian General Assembly, sending Scottish Presbyterians into decline for a time. While Cromwell governed England under the Protectorate, he continued political developments that moved England irreversibly toward constitutional monarchy.

Many of the English, Scots, and Irish did not like Cromwell. When he died, they assisted in the reestablishment of the Stuart King, Charles II, in 1660. Dissenters such as Presbyterians and Congregationalists did not fare well during the Restoration, however. Presbyterianism, it was said, was not a "religion for gentlemen." Many dissenters gave up their state stipends rather than their Christian convictions. Persons such as Richard Baxter (1615–1691) made notable contributions to British religious life. Baxter, who shared Presbyterian ideas, was a supporter of associations and ecumenical cooperation even with the Anglicans. He influenced future generations of Calvinists with *The Reformed Pastor* (1656), where he instructed the minister to preach "as a dying man to dying men [and women]." In *The Christian Directory* (1673), Baxter offered a monumental collection of reflections on the Christian responsibility in social, political, and economic life. In *The Saints' Everlasting Rest* (1650) he described the Christian's ultimate hope in Christ. Dissenters, such as Baxter, were unable to attend educational institutions of the Anglican establishment and could not hold official ecclesiastical or governmental positions because of their nonconformity. However, they did become leaders in England's economic development.

Discontent grew in the British Isles when James II succeeded Charles. The king had overt Roman Catholic sympathies and attempted to impose episcopacy on the Scots, who resented royal absolutism. He thus succeeded by his actions in reinvigorating Scottish Presbyterians and in angering the English. By the 1680s the English were ready to turn to William and Mary of the Reformed Church in the Netherlands. William and Mary were named sovereign by an act of the British Parliament to succeed the last Stuart. The "Glorious Revolution" occurred peacefully in 1688. While William and Mary continued the Anglican communion as the established church of the realm, these constitutional monarchs also implemented some Puritan political ideas. Among the first things that the Parliament did under the reign of William and Mary was to adopt the Toleration Act of 1689, which granted toleration to dissenters. In defense of this move, John Locke wrote *A Letter concerning Toleration* (1689). Locke, who lived in exile in the Netherlands, was an English Whig with Calvinist sympathies. He wanted limitations on the authority and power of the monarchy. In his famous *Letter*, he argued that "toleration" is the "chief characteristic mark of the true church." The Gospel of Jesus Christ is based on "faith which works, not by force, but by love." This was an important step toward the end of the religious conflict in England, on the way toward religious freedom for all British subjects. At this time the Presbyterian Church of Scotland was granted full legal recognition. Under the Heads of Agreement (1691), Congregationalists and Presbyterians in England and Scotland began to cooperate again on matters of common concern. In England, however, Presbyterian faith and life grew weaker for a time.

Presbyterians in Ireland

Ireland, with its Roman Catholic population, did not escape the conflicts in England and Scotland. The Irish were often manipulated by European powers such as Rome, France, and Spain in their struggles with England. Ireland presented a problem for Elizabeth, who confiscated Irish lands and was one of the first to use the term "Scotch-Irish" to deal with the Scot immigration to the island. James I wanted to bring Ireland under control and consequently implemented a plantation system with immigrants from England and southwestern Scotland. The Scots settled the "Plantation of Ulster" in Northern Ireland, taking with them their Presbyterian commitments. Although the Anglican church enjoyed the authority and power of supremacy in Ireland, most of the citizens were Roman Catholics, Presbyterians, or the unchurched from Scotland. Bishop James Ussher, Irish himself, was a Calvinist and preferred a synodical government in the Church of England. Presbyterian faith and life was vigorous despite the attempt of Charles I to curb the Presbyterian community in Ireland.

The tensions between the Irish and the English grew during the seventeenth century. Irish Catholics, long resentful of the English, revolted in 1641 and massacred many of the Protestant immigrants. To protect their countrymen abroad, the Scots sent ten thousand troops to help Cromwell check and suppress this insurrection. Along with the troops, the Scots sent chaplains. Out of this army, with its regiments organized as church congregations, emerged the first presbytery of 1642. Within a few years there were eighty congregations with one hundred thousand members in the Presbyterian Church in Ulster. Irish Presbyterians did not approve of the execution of Charles I, and thus some were subject to reprisals of Cromwell's policies. In general, however, Cromwell's policies were benevolent with regard to Protestants. At the Restoration of the monarchy in England, Charles II made Irish Presbyterians suffer as dissenters in much the same way as the Roman Catholics. They were denied financial support for churches, political positions, and even the right to attend Trinity College in Dublin. Francis Makemie, born in Ramelton, Ireland (ca. 1658–1717), so important for the development of Presbyterian faith and life in America, had to leave Ireland for Scotland to study at the University of Glasgow before he could be ordained by the Irish Presbytery of Laggan.

James II was a Catholic and had no zeal for making Presbyterians into Episcopalians. But to bolster his political power, he extended some freedom to non-Anglican groups—Presbyterians and Roman Catholics—in Ireland. He placed the Irish army under Roman Catholic officers. The Catholics then threatened Protestants in an extended siege of Derry. William of Orange, the new King of England, and leader of the Protestant army, lifted the siege and defeated the deposed James II at the Battle of the Boyne. This effectively ended James' power and that of his Roman Catholic supporters. These battles, however, did not resolve the Irish problem. Indeed, these ancient battles are still remembered by some as though they occurred only yesterday.

Ireland and Scotland were annexed politically to the British Isles. With the ascendancy of William and Mary to the throne of England religious conflict did abate. In this connection, when William addressed the General Assembly of the Church of Scotland, he suggested that "moderation" was now needed. Later, during Queen Anne's reign, the Act of Security safeguarded Presbyterians in the north as the parliaments of the two countries were united in 1707. However, the Patronage Act gave to aristocrats who controlled church property the right to present ministers to parishes, thus undercutting one of the prerogatives of congregations to elect their own pastors. This created new tensions for Presbyterians. During these years, Protestants of all varieties were reminded often of repressive acts portrayed in John Foxe's *Acts and Monuments Happening in the Church.* In his enormously popular and often reprinted book, *Foxe's Book of Martyrs* (1563), he depicted the ugly persecution of earlier centuries during the age of the Tudors and Stuarts. Thus the stage was set for the swarming of Presbyterians from Ireland and Scotland to the New World in the eighteenth century.

4

The First American Presbytery and an "Errand into the Wilderness"

The Reverend Francis Makemie (d. 1708), an Ulster Scot immigrant to the American wilderness, often has been referred to as the "Father of American Presbyterians." He settled on the eastern shore of Virginia in 1683, planting churches in Maryland, as well as Virginia. Moreover, Makemie played a leading role in organizing the first presbytery in Philadelphia in 1706. In a letter to London in 1709 the new presbytery explained that it had organized to better manage "Evangelical Affairs." It implored help in providing ministers for people "crying" for the "word of life" in the American wilderness.

Presbyterians were among the earliest Reformed immigrants to America. This Reformed exodus from Europe to America took place as the British continued to compete with Spain, Portugal, and France for land throughout the world, in this case in the western hemisphere. English defeat of the Spanish Armada in 1588 stimulated this competition. English geographer, Richard Hakluyt wrote *The Principal Navigations, Voyages, Traffiques, and Discoveries of the English Nation* (1598–1600) and clergyman, Samuel Purchas wrote *His Pilgrimage* (1613), both travel literature that told about the adventures, explorations, and early colonization of various parts of the world. The authors set forth motivations for this errand into the American wilderness. These promoted the glory of God, the Reformed religion, the honor of the king, profit, and relief of the population explosion in England. So began the British conquest and occupation of North America, the growth of the thirteen original British colonies, and a western trek to the Pacific coast. Although Roman Catholics, Lutherans, and other religious groups may be found in the early European migration, Calvinists of Anglican, Huguenots, Dutch and German, Congregationalists, and Presbyterian persuasions dominated this early colonization process.

Immigration and Settlement

The low church Anglicans settled in Jamestown in 1607 and organized a congregation sympathetic toward Puritan interests. Anglicans soon extended the established church in places such as Virginia, New York, the Carolinas, and Maryland. French Calvinists also came to the colonies and settled up and down the eastern seacoast. Because of Anglican tolerance, some of them joined that denomination. After the Dutch had been defeated for control of the New York area of the country, the English tolerated the Dutch Reformed along the Hudson and in Jersey. Puritan Congregationalists established themselves in New England, especially in Massachusetts and Connecticut, where Puritans thought of themselves as a "City upon a Hill" and a shining example of the New World to the Old World. The German Reformed settled in William Penn's Philadelphia and Pennsylvania, as well as Jersey, where they depended on the Dutch for help in their religious developments.

From the beginning, immigrants with Presbyterian affiliations and sympathies settled up and down the eastern seacoast in all the colonies and then began to push westward into the American wilderness. They arrived in the southern colonies and settled along the Elizabeth, Potomac, and James Rivers. By the 1690s they had organized a church in Norfolk. They also settled in Maryland and Delaware around the Chesapeake Bay. A considerable number of Presbyterians settled in New England between the 1625s and 1640s, although they were sometimes congregationalized in those early years. Those who settled in Connecticut maintained their Presbyterian sympathies. Some Presbyterians immigrated to the Carolinas and established congregations in Charleston as early as the seventeenth century. Most Presbyterians, however, sailed to the middle colonies of New York, New Jersey, and Pennsylvania, where they enjoyed toleration, for the most part, by government authorities. Congregations were organized on Long Island as early as the 1640s in Southhold and Southampton. New England Presbyterians founded congregations in New Jersey. The First Presbyterian Church was finally organized in the City of Brotherly Love in 1701 by Jedediah Andrews, a graduate of Harvard College.

Of all the early Presbyterian pioneers, we know most about Makemie, who was born in Ramelton, Ireland, about the year 1658. Because of restrictions by the Anglican establishment on Presbyterians, as well as Roman Catholics, in the seventeenth century, Makemie had to return to Scotland for his theological education. After graduating from the University of Glasgow, he was ordained by the Presbytery of Laggan in Ireland and sent to the colonies as a missionary, first to the Barbados and then to the eastern shore. Makemie authored a number of pamphlets. In *An Answer to George Keith's Libel Against a Catechism* (1694) he defended the authority of the Bible and Reformed theology against an itinerant Quaker named George Keith, who had once been a Presbyterian. In 1697, while visiting the Barbados, he wrote another pamphlet titled *Truth in a True Light,* which was published in 1699. In this pamphlet he argued that Presbyterians and Anglicans share many of the same theological opinions, even though they may differ in some aspects of worship, governance, and discipline. He also called attention to the fact that Anglicans recognized the legitimacy of Presbyterian practices in Old England under the Toleration Act, which was just recently enacted under William and Mary. Makemie, although somewhat abrasive in this writing, expressed the hope that such ecumenism would be practiced in the New World under different circumstances. In his defense of Presbyterian dissent from the Anglican establishment, he appealed to Jesus and his disciples as the first Christian dissenters.

Makemie had established himself on the eastern shore and later married Naomi Anderson, daughter of William Anderson, a wealthy merchant and landholder in Accomax. The Makemies had two daughters, neither of whom had any children. In addition to being a minister, Makemie became a merchant, as well as a farmer and a slave holder. He also traveled south to the Carolinas and as far north as Boston where he preached on behalf of Reformed faith and life. His congregation in Rehoboth, Maryland, is still an active congregation. In another pamphlet, *A Plain and Friendly Persuasive to the Inhabitants of Virginia and Maryland, for Promoting Towns and Cohabitation* (1705), he encouraged the building of communities with churches and schools in order to promote morality and literacy. He also encouraged economic development for the public good. In his several pamphlets, Makemie treated subjects of theology, worship, governance, and the public good, to which American Presbyterians would continually return in later years.

The First Presbytery and the Right to Preach

Some Presbyterian ministers met in Philadelphia in 1706 "to consult the most proper measure for advancing religion and propagating Christianity" in the American wilderness. They formed the Presbytery of Philadelphia, the first Presbyterian presbytery of the New World. Although the first page of minutes is missing, the conferees seemed to follow the procedures of the Church of Scotland in this organizational process. The body, however, was independent of any foreign ecclesiastical institution. It was formed to meet the needs of those people in the "desolate places" of the American colonies. Moreover, presbytery members represented a multicultural mix from the very beginning, albeit all from the British Isles: John Andrews was from England; John Wilson and A. N. Taylor from New England; George McNish immigrated from Scotland; and John Hampton along with Samuel Davie represented the Scotch-Irish. Francis Makemie also was from Ireland. Welsh pastors Howell Powell and Malachi Jones soon associated with the organization. Laymen John Yard, William Smith, John Gardner, and James Stoddard joined the clergy at the second meeting of the body.

As indicated in the minutes, members gathered for moral support, for deepening their faith, for disciplining members, for stimulating professional development, and to examine candidates for ordination. They also gathered to set goals for the presbytery and Presbyterians. At the first meeting, the presbytery examined and ordained John Boyd to the ministry. It heard him preach on John 1:12: "But to all who received him . . . [God] gave power to become children of God," first with an exegesis of the text, then exposition followed by application. This represented the proper composition of the sermon for Presbyterian pulpits. In the second meeting, the enlarged assembly adopted the following goals:

> Overtures proposed to the Presbytery & agreed upon, for propagating the interest of religion:
>
> First that evry minister in their respective congregations read & comment upon a chapter of the bible every Lords day, as discretion [and] ye circumstance of tyme, place, & c. will admit.
>
> Second over: that it be recommended to evry minister of the Presbytery to set on foot & encourage private christian societies.
>
> Third over: That evry minister of the Presbytery supplie neighbouring desolate places where a minister is wanting & opportunity of doing good offers.

Meeting in Philadelphia, Presbyterian clergy assumed the freedom to organize and the right to worship, to preach and teach, and to administer the sacraments. Presbyterians made no divine right claims of Presbyterian order or for an establishment of the Presbyterian Church. They could not assume such rights in other colonies where the Anglican Church was established. When Makemie arrived as a Presbyterian missionary in the New World, he obtained a license to preach, demonstrating his respect for the law and the civil magistrate. When he and a colleague traveled to New York, just after the meeting of the presbytery, they were forbidden to preach in a church by Lord Cornbury, a relative of Queen Anne and governor of the colony. Makemie's reputation had arrived in New York before he did. He was thought of as a Presbyterian "bishop," going around ordaining ministers and making a "great noise" wherever he traveled. Governor Cornbury wrote that Makemie was a "Jack of all Trades; he is a preacher, a Doctor of Physics, a Merchant, an attorney, or Counselor at Law, and which is worst of all, a Disturber of Government. . . ."

Cornbury held that the Toleration Act of 1689 did not apply to the colonies. Makemie argued that it did and, moreover, he held a license to preach. When he was forbidden to preach in a church building, he disobeyed the law publicly, showing a willingness to bear the penalty for his act. He went into a private house, opened the doors and windows, and carried out his ministerial function so that all could see and hear and participate if they so desired. Confronted by this act of civil disobedience, Cornbury arrested Makemie and his colleague and brought Makemie to trial. Makemie obtained a writ of *habeas corpus*. He insisted that the Governor produce and show the court in writing the law that sanctioned the Governor's abuse. Cornbury could not do this, and Makemie won his case. For his defiance, however, he spent forty-six days in jail, and he was forced to pay his expenses while in custody, as well as the cost of the trial. The Presbyterian minister immediately published *A Narrative of a New and Unusual American Imprisonment* (1707), and he emerged a hero among dissenters, no matter what Lord Cornbury thought of him.

Building Up
the Body of Christ

Presbyterians grew in numbers as immigrants continued to flow from Europe. The presbytery organized itself into a Synod of Philadelphia in 1716, growing organizationally from the bottom up. The synod then divided into four presbyteries—Philadelphia, New Castle, Long Island, and Snow Hill, although the last was never organized. Beginning about that time, Presbyterians from Northern Ireland immigrated in the greatest number, although not all the Scotch-Irish were Presbyterian. First of all, although treated better in Ireland under Queen Anne than under other monarchs, Presbyterians, like Roman Catholics, suffered economic and political, as well as religious, disadvantages under an Anglican establishment. Second, the Irish suffered economically when landlords raised the rents for their lands. Economic dislocation and distress affected numerous families, and many of them immigrated. Wave after wave of these immigrants braved voyages in 1717–1718, 1727–1728, 1740–1741,

1754–1755, and 1771–1775, until approximately 250,000 had crossed the Atlantic; nobody knows the exact number. Some entered New Jersey and Pennsylvania by way of Philadelphia. They often moved west toward what became Pittsburgh, or south by way of the Valley of Virginia, where they settled, or pressed on to the Carolina back country. As they suffered and sometimes died in their exodus from Ireland, so they experienced hardship in their new homeland in an untamed wilderness. They made life more dangerous for themselves by encroaching on Indian territory. Some of them not religiously affiliated found their way into Baptist, and later, Methodist churches for solace and help. Many joined the growing Presbyterian Church. Whereas some Scots immigrated in those early years, their numbers did not increase until later in the century.

Appealing to Old England and New England for help, the synod attempted to supply ministerial leadership, and tried to maintain ministerial standards. Although some were trained in British institutions or at Harvard or Yale, most clergy were taught and served apprenticeships under experienced pastors. Presbyteries examined candidates before ordination on knowledge of learned languages, on the exegesis of the Scriptures in Latin, and on resourcefulness in preaching. Presbyteries disciplined ministers also. Alexander Hutchison, so the minutes report, was censured by New Castle Presbytery for bathing on the Lord's Day. Presbyterians had to face misconduct of church members also, making the New World not much better than the Old by their conduct. One clergyman wrote back to Scotland:

> There are a great many young men merch[ants] who come from your parts, soberly (I believe) educated and brought up at home, who, when they arive [sic] here are meer rakes, stop or stand at no sin or vice almost that falls in their way, swearing, whoring, Sabbath breaking, drunkenness, are as common vices, with a great many of them, as if they tho't there wos [sic] no evil in the commission of any of these . . .

The immigrants, according to the correspondent, were a disgrace to the homeland and a "perfect scandal to all religion" in America. In the eighteenth century, clergy and sessions had their hands full serving as moral courts in the American wilderness in the absence of any organized civil life.

The synod confronted the intellectual challenges emanating from the Enlightenment and its religious expression in Deism. This movement was spreading even among members of the church. Deists believed in God the Creator of nature and nature's uniform laws. They used the image of a clockmaker and the mechanism of a clock to describe God and God's work. They also had trouble dealing with evil and human sinfulness. But they denied other aspects of God's relation to believers, such as Redeemer and Provider. They also rejected the Bible as the rule of Christian faith and life, as well as doctrinal standards such as the *Westminster Confession* and catechisms.

Because of this dispute, the Irish church required that clergy subscribe to the *Westminster Standards*. This development influenced the Synod of Philadelphia. The Reverend Jonathan Dickinson (1688–1747), a New Englander who became a Presbyterian pastor in the Middle Colonies, expressed uneasiness about the direction the church was taking in Ireland. As early as 1722 he suggested that all authority for Christian faith and life is derived from Jesus Christ as revealed in the Bible. He honored the *Westminster Confession*. As one of the earliest Presbyterian theologians, he wrote defenses of Calvinism and the confession. But he was uneasy about an act that seemed to place the work of the Westminster Assembly on an equal footing with the Bible. He reminded his readers of the claims of the Roman Catholics for the teaching authority of the church and the Canons of the Council of Trent that had so troubled the earliest Protestants. The Reverend John Thomson argued that a denomination without a confessional standard was like a "city without walls." He wished to protect Presbyterians from the pernicious attacks of Deists on Christian faith and life. Therefore all clergy should subscribe to the *Westminster Confession* and catechisms as the expression of their beliefs and agree, under a public vow to preach and teach such doctrine, as they did in Ireland. In 1727 New Castle Presbytery asked the synod to take Thompson's position rather than that of Dickinson.

The synod engaged in a lengthy debate. Then it agreed to what was called the "Adopting Act" of 1729, which set a pattern for American Presbyterians in theological disputes. The parties agreed to an accommodation. In the act, the synod disclaimed any attempt to legislate the conscience and declared Christ and the Bible as the source and rule of Christian faith and life. It then described the *Westminster Confession* and the catechisms "as being in all essential and necessary articles, good forms of sound words and systems of Christian doctrine." It also required that all members of presbyteries verbally assent to these documents. The synod then provided for a way of "scrupling," that is, of allowing those who wished to do so to express any disagreement with the standards. The ordaining body would decide if disagreements fell outside the parameters set by the "necessary and essential" articles. On the same day this act was adopted, members of the synod gave an example of this approach. They agreed that the relation of the civil magistrate to the church, as defined by the Westminster Assembly in the 1640s, was not "essential and necessary" for Christian faith and life in the American colonies. This article had given the civil magistrate the right to call ecclesiastical meetings and to intervene in church affairs. Perhaps members of synod recalled at this point Francis Makemie's experience with Lord Cornbury in New York. So Presbyterians weathered their first theological conflict by accommodating several values for the good of the larger body. This approach was tested further as synod and presbyteries welcomed new immigrants, built new churches, tried to meet Christian need, and tamed the American wilderness.

5

Spiritual Awakening, Leadership, and Reunion

During the years between the 1730s and the American Revolution, Presbyterians sank roots deep in the American soil, experienced spiritual awakening, built institutions, developed leadership, and mended their first division. In letters sent to supporters in the British Isles, colonists continued to ask for trained leaders to help minister to the thousands of immigrants swarming to the New World from Ireland, Scotland, and England. Presbyterians from the New York and New Jersey area appealed for such help for Pennsylvania, Maryland, Virginia, and the Carolinas, as well as for themselves. "A great number of congregations have been formed upon the Presbyterian plan," they reported, and the people needed the "ministrations of the gospel." Philadelphia Presbyterians also wrote to Britain, asking not only for church leaders but also for help to support them and their families while congregational life took shape. Life was precarious in America's "wide extended Wilderness" and on its various "frontiers." They wanted funds to be administered by a Charitable Corporation for ministerial families while Presbyterians extended the "Bounds of Christ's Kingdom" and the "British Empire in America."

As the Reformed tradition took root in the American colonies, Presbyterians had their hands full helping immigrants adjust to life. In their synod and presbyteries, they had to sort out tensions that grew from spiritual ferment and that led to what was called the New Side–Old Side division. They began to develop their own educational, mission, and charitable institutions, out of which grew remarkable indigenous leadership. After mending their division, they found themselves involved in a conflict of the British Empire called the French and Indian War. At the same time, they began to experience some discontent with and independence from the mother country.

Spiritual Awakening

At the same time American Presbyterians were discussing the Adopting Act of 1729, they were facing a tension deep in the Reformed tradition between the life of the heart and that of the mind. Earlier Reformers attempted to hold these aspects of Christian faith and life together. Calvin, a child of the Renaissance, embraced the new learning of his age, while at the same time insisting that Christians could only understand God's will and ways in the Scriptures through the testimony of the Holy Spirit in the heart. The writers of the *Westminster Confession* in the 1640s, while embracing aspects of the Age of Reason, maintained that believers could only know the message of redemption through the "inward work of the Holy Spirit, bearing witness by and with the word" in their hearts. In the eighteenth century, an Age of Enlightenment, Christians in the Reformed tradition experienced spiritual quickenings called "Pietism" among the Dutch and Germans, "Methodism" among the British, and the "Great Awakening" among the American colonialists. Anglican clergyman George Whitefield (1714–1770), a graduate of Oxford, holding Calvinist theology, using Methodist tactics, influenced American Presbyterians during his colonial itineracy. One English actor commented that Whitefield's preaching was so persuasive that he could make people weep by the way he pronounced "Mesopotamia." Although Presbyterians attempted to hold the head and heart together, to do things decently and in order, sometimes things got out of hand.

A New Side and Old Side emerged during this controversy. The New Side supported the Awakening developed through the work of William Tennent and his sons, William and Gilbert. Father Tennent, an Irish clergyman, converted from Anglicanism to the Presbyterian Church. He did not approve of episcopacy, that is, the government of the church by bishops. Desiring to develop leadership for Presbyterians in the middle colonies, he formed a "Log College" in Neshaminy, Pennsylvania, so his sons could be educated without going to Harvard, Yale, or William and Mary, or returning to Europe. He nurtured his students' piety as well as their heads. While Tennent taught only a few men, Whitefield was so impressed with the results that he claimed "Log College" graduates turned the "world upside down." The Reverend Gilbert Tennent (1703–1764), a "son of thunder," certainly disturbed the church with his contentious sermon, titled "The Dangers of an Unconverted Ministry" (1740). He proclaimed, broadside, that the Presbyterian ministers did not know Christ. They were not shepherds, but "Pharisee-Teachers," "dead dogs," the blind leading the blind. As he censored the clergy, he encouraged people to leave "dead" congregations to join other congregations for soul-food. Tennent himself preached in parishes not his own, to provide such spiritual nourishment. At about the same time, the Reverend Jonathan Edwards (1703–1758) of Northampton, Massachusetts, delivered another sermon titled "Sinners in the Hands of an Angry God" (1741). The brilliant Edwards, who began his ministry in the Presbyterian church of New York, had a profound piety, and was encouraged and nurtured by his wife Sarah, who shared his sense of the sovereign holiness of God. In his sermon he urged his congregants to convert. He warned them that they were suspended over hell fire, held only by the thread of a spider's web. He emphasized their dependence on the grace of God, and reminded them of justification by faith alone. The Reverend Samuel Blair, a graduate of the Log College, as was William Tennent, urged his hearers to have "faith in Christ," to "close with Christ," to "adventure life upon Christ." New Side clergy observed the impact their preaching had on their hearers, and they were concerned about some of its effects.

Old Side members of the denomination were alarmed by what they called "enthusiasm" as well as "censoriousness" and "itineracy." All this was disruptive of congregational and personal life and growth. Old Siders were disturbed by incidents of weeping, screaming, fainting, bodily commotions like "epileptic fits," which indicated loss of control accompanying some awakening preaching. This kind of behavior did not manifest the gracious work of God's Spirit. They were also deeply troubled by accusations, such as those of Gilbert Tennent, that they were "graceless." Consequently, Old Side members of the Synod of Philadelphia decided to go their own way in 1741. This denominational division led to the formation of the New Side Synod of New York. The Awakening and its consequences caused considerable reflection on the nature of Reformed piety, which Jonathan Edwards explored in his work *Religious Affections* (1744). In it he attempted to show the wholeness of the Christian personality, and to commend genuinely wholesome Christian conversion and wholesome Christian life measured by biblical criteria. Even before the division of 1741, Presbyterians, New Side and Old Side, had begun to build institutions fostering education, missions, and charitable causes, especially for Presbyterian pastors and their families.

Institutions for Education, Mission, and Charity

Presbyterians, as indicated by William Tennent who founded the Log College, recognized the need for and founded other educational academies in the Middle colonies. The New Side leader, Jonathan Dickinson, gave continuity to Tennent's Log College by securing a charter from New Jersey to form a college in his home in Elizabethtown, New Jersey. This institution moved to Princeton in 1746, where it became the College of New Jersey and evolved later into Princeton University. Old Side members of the Synod of Philadelphia also took the educational challenge seriously, organizing the Synodical Academy of New London, Pennsylvania, under the leadership of Francis Alison. This effort contributed to the founding of the College of Philadelphia, an ecumenical adventure involving Anglicans. Alison was a principal instructor at the College, and had the reputation of being the finest classical scholar in America. Presbyterian laymen William Livingston, William Smith, and John Morin Scott, all lawyers, encouraged the founding of Kings College in New York. But they insisted in their *Independent Reflector* that it be open to all youth and under ecumenical auspices, not under Anglican domination. In New York, as well as in Philadelphia and Princeton, Presbyterians passed on biblical and classical learning, and trained clergy and citizens for the American colonial life.

Although still cooperating with the British and New Englanders, American Presbyterians began to support their own evangelization of Native Americans and African Americans. David Brainerd, a protégé of Edwards, illustrates the concern for Indians. Brainerd attended Yale College and responded positively to the Awakening. He once impertinently informed a skeptical instructor that the latter had no more grace than the chair on which he was sitting. For this insult, the college refused to grant the upstart student a degree. Nevertheless, Brainerd was ordained by the New Side Presbyterians in New York as a missionary to the Delaware Indians. Although dying of tuberculosis, he crossed over into the "howling wilderness," as he put it, between the Delaware and the Susquehanna Rivers, to preach to his "beloved" native people. While condemning pernicious habits and idolatry, his practice of the presence of God and his preaching, even through an interpreter—according to his account—made a deep impression on the Indians. His memoir, *An Account of the Life of the Late David Brainerd* (1749), edited by Edwards after Brainerd's death, motivated men and women to volunteer for mission service and to support missions well into the next century.

In the north, Eleazer Wheelock, a New England Congregationalist minister, organized a school for Indians, which eventually merged with Dartmouth College. He trained Native American Samson Occum, who was ordained by Suffolk Presbytery as a missionary to the Mohegan tribe. Occum made a trip to England and Scotland to solicit funds for Indian education. He was a "curiosity" wherever he preached. Anglican bishops did not attract him. They gave the impression that they did not want to share heaven with Native Americans. In the south, the Reverend Samuel Davies was concerned about evangelizing the Indians on the Virginia and Carolina frontier. He solicited funds for the work, although his efforts did not bear much fruit there. Settlers pushing Native Americans westward compromised those evangelical efforts and stirred Indian resistance to this process of occupation and evangelization. Davies was more effective in his work among slaves in Virginia. He provided them with literature and encouraged them to learn and to teach each other to read. He was moved by their singing of hymns and also distributed hymnbooks among them in order to comfort them with Christian faith and hope. Davies did not challenge the institution of slavery itself.

Ministers faced hardships and dangers as they traveled with immigrants moving westward into the wilderness. As in the east, so in the west, clergy and their families had to deal with uncertainties and even calamities. Life was precarious as Presbyterians attempted to bring order out of chaos that was often connected with the frontier. In the Ohio country, missionary Charles Beatty, for example, wrote about preaching to people crowded into a little house because of the rain. While preaching, a rattlesnake crept into the house, causing alarm among the people. Fortunately, it was killed before it could do any damage, as was another snake discovered at the same time. Meanwhile, in the Carolina back country, an observer described the "Riots, Frolics, Races, Games, Cards, Dice, Dances," along with the "Intemperance and Intoxication of both sexes, Young and Old," which led to "Strifes, Contentions, Variance, Dissimulations, Envyings, Slanders, Backbitings, and a thousand other Evils" such as "Fighting, Brawling, Gouging, [and] Quarreling." This description may have involved some hyperbole, but it expressed some of the hazards that Presbyterian ministers and their families had to face in ministering in such places. The Synod of Philadelphia took the lead in providing some security for ministers who were concerned about their wives and children, as well as themselves, under such precarious conditions. It did so by organizing the Corporation for the Relief of Poor and Distressed Presbyterian Ministers. While doing this, the Synod also appealed to British Christians to support ministers and their families who were risking their lives in the wilderness so that "Christ's kingdom" and the "British Empire" might root, grow, and flourish. Out of this early charity, the Presbyterian pension plan emerged, known until recently as The Presbyterian Ministers' Fund. This was America's first life insurance company.

Indigenous Leaders

From these early roots an indigenous Presbyterian leadership grew. In addition to New York laymen such as Livingston, Smith, and Scott, Benjamin Franklin, a Congregationalist while in Boston but a Presbyterian when he first settled in Philadelphia, transferred to the Anglican Church when he became fed up with the doctrinal disputes between Old Side–New Side Presbyterians. Physicians John Redmon and Benjamin Rush, both Presbyterian elders, practiced medicine in Philadelphia. They expressed concern for the cure of the soul as well as the body in their practices. Clergymen Jonathan Dickinson (preacher-educator), Gilbert Tennent, Samuel Blair, Francis Alison, Jonathan Edwards, and Samuel Davies already have been introduced. Edwards and Davies emerged as colonial leaders whose theology and preaching gained for them trans-Atlantic reputations.

Edwards maintained Presbyterian sympathies and was much admired by Presbyterians, while pastor of the Congregational Church, Northampton, Massachusetts. He gained his reputation as a theologian in his attempt to sort out the genuine marks of the work of God's Holy Spirit in defense of the Awakening of the 1730s and 1740s. Because of conflict within his congregation, he took his family to Stockbridge in 1751, where he served as missionary to Native Americans. While there, he produced the notable works *Freedom of the Will* (1754) and *The Nature of True Virtue* (1765), in which he attempted to defend the sovereignty of God. He also produced an Augustinian work, *A History of the Work of Redemption,* published posthumously, finding a place for the New World in God's redemptive plans. He claimed to be a theologian of "justification by faith alone" and stressed God's sovereignty in the work of redemption. In *God Glorified in the Work of Redemption, by the Greatness of Man's Dependence Upon Him in the Whole of It* (1731), he wrote of God's sovereignty: "There is an Absolute and universal dependence of the Redeemed on God. . . . The redeemed are in everything directly, immediately, and entirely dependent on God. . . ." He also held that God is in us and with us, as he did in his great work on *The Religious Affections* (1746):

> He who has no religious affection, is in a state of spiritual death, and is wholly destitute of the powerful, quickening, saving influences of the Spirit of God upon his heart. As there is no true religion where there is nothing else but affection, so there is no true religion where there is no religious affection. As on the one hand, there must be light in the understanding, as well as an affected fervent heart; where there is heat without light, there can be nothing divine or heavenly in that heart; so on the other hand, where there is a kind of light without heat, a head stored with notions and speculations, with a

cold and unaffected heart, there can be nothing divine in that light, that knowledge is no true spiritual knowledge of divine things. If the great things of religion are rightly understood, they will affect the heart. The reason why men are not affected by such infinitely great, important, glorious, and wonderful things, as they often hear and read of, in the word of God, is undoubtedly because they are blind; if they were not so, it would be impossible, and utterly inconsistent with human nature, that their hearts should be otherwise than strongly impressed, and greatly moved by such things.

Edwards was invited to be President of the College of New Jersey in Princeton. He died of a smallpox inoculation shortly after settling there in 1758.

Samuel Davies (1723–1761), one of the most eloquent and persuasive preachers in the colonies, was Welsh. Trained and ordained for the ministry in Pennsylvania, he went south to Virginia. There he was successful in organizing Hanover Presbytery by 1755, shortly after he began his ministry. He registered for a license to preach at Presbyterian meeting houses within the Anglican establishment in Virginia, thus obeying the law. But he argued for his right to organize other congregations and to preach and to itinerate under the Toleration Act. He visited Britain with Gilbert Tennent to raise funds for the College of New Jersey. While abroad, he preached before King George II. To bring sinners to Christ, Davies preached eloquently. Exploring Acts 17:30, where God "commandeth all men everywhere to repent," Davies proclaimed:

> This command, therefore is binding upon you all. The Great God cries to you all, *Repent!* Repent, young and old, rich and poor, white and black, free and bond:—Repent, ye young sinners, now while your hearts are soft and tender, and your passions easily moved, and you are not hardened by a long course of habitual sinning; Repent, ye greyheaded veteran sinners, now at least repent, when the load of sins, heaped up for so many years, lies so heavy upon you, and you are walking every moment on the slippery brink of eternity: Repent, ye rich men; ye are not above this command: Repent, ye poor; ye are not beneath it: Repent ye poor slaves; your color, or low state in life, cannot free you from this command: Repent, ye masters, for your sins against your Master, who is in heaven. In short, God commandeth all men, kings and subject, the highest and the lowest, and all the intermediate ranks, to repent.

Davies believed that it was only by such preaching that men and women could be brought into the churches. He opposed the use of force by the secular authority to make people attend and pay for religious services.

Such coercion, he maintained in another sermon, only produced "hypocrites." He concluded that the "weapons of the apostolic warfare, which were so mighty through God, were miracles, reasoning, entreaty, and the love of a crucified Savior; and these were adapted to the nature of the human mind, to subdue it without violence, and sweetly captivate every thought into obedience to Christ." His preaching illustrates the leveling effect of the Awakening and how he was willing to trust in the art of persuasion rather than the coercion of church establishments to strengthen religion. Samuel Davies succeeded Edwards as President at Princeton in 1758. Never in good health, Davies died at the early age of thirty-eight.

The leaven of the Enlightenment as well as the Awakening seemed to stimulate women to a new assertiveness. Esther Burr (1732–1758) was Edwards' daughter and the husband of Aaron Burr, who was also president of Princeton before Edwards or Davies. Esther shows that the leveling experiences of both the Enlightenment and the Evangelical Awakening were having an influence on women. Esther recounts in her journal how she entered into "sharp combat" with a tutor at the College of New Jersey. He claimed that a little learning made women proud, and that women did not know anything about true friendship and society. Esther reports that she rebutted this contention and confused the young man. He ended the conversation abruptly and departed from her company. She does not report if she persuaded him that women were every bit the equal of men.

Reunion, War, and
Stirrings of Independence

In 1758 Presbyterians reunited, healing the breach of 1741 between the Synod of New York and the Synod of Philadelphia. The attempt to overcome this division started shortly after it occurred through the expressions of regrets by those on both sides. Gilbert Tennent, for example, infamous for his "censoriousness" and "itineracy," wrote an ecumenical tract titled *Irenicum Ecclesiasticum* (1745), which expressed his deep concern over divisions in the church. He called for union and cooperation among Christians. Tennent also became the pastor of a prominent church in Philadelphia during those years in the bosom of the Old Side party. In a Plan of Reunion of 1758, both Synods agreed to form the Synod of New York and Philadelphia. They accepted the *Westminster Confession* and *Larger* and *Shorter Catechisms* as "an orthodox and excellent system of Christian doctrine, founded on the word of God . . ." together with the *Directory of Worship* and the discipline that they had inherited from the Reformed community in the British Isles. They pledged to conduct church meetings decently and in order, allowing freedom of discussion and protest. They also provided for peaceable withdrawal from the body should someone not agree with the judgment of the governing bodies of the church. In other accommodations, they agreed to ask candidates to the ministry to give satisfaction as to "learning and experimental acquaintance with religion, and skill in divinity and cases of conscience," together with the acceptance of the doctrinal standards of the church. With regard to the most recent controversy over the Awakening, the synod gave thanks for every manifestation of the work of God's Spirit among Presbyterians during the previous years. It gave thanks for persons who showed evidence of conviction of sin and conscious conversion, followed by the assurance of God's acceptance. This particular order of salvation was not sanctioned by the synod as the only order of Christian experience for all members of the church. Furthermore, the synod warned against uncritically accepting some of the extreme experiences of the Awakening as scriptural signs of grace. The synod urged members to accept one another with a judgment of charity in gauging a Christian's orthodoxy and experience. While some may have entered this ecclesiastical arrangement cautiously, others rejoiced over the reunion of the denomination.

This reunion took place as American colonists became embroiled in the war of the British against the French—known as the French and Indian War or the Seven Years' War—in which Presbyterians found themselves in frontier engagements with Indians stirred up by the French. Native Americans were already aroused by colonial encroachment on western lands. Presbyterians such as Samuel Davies viewed the war as just, being fought in defense against a major Roman Catholic power and against the fierce "savages" of the American wilderness. The British won the war and removed the French, though not the Native Americans, as a danger to colonists.

Along with Presbyterians from Ireland who immigrated in great numbers during those years, the Scottish Presbyterians also sailed to America and increased Reformed ranks. In the early years of the eighteenth century, the Scottish Presbyterian Church suffered several divisions, small ones having to do with the obligation of Presbyterians to renew Scottish covenants made in times of persecution and conflict with England. Known as Covenanters and Seceders, these immigrants formed an associate presbytery in 1753. One of these Covenanters, Alexander Craighead, joined a New Side presbytery. In 1742 he insisted that his presbytery renew the Scottish National Covenant of 1581 and the Solemn League and Covenant, which opposed the incorporation of Scotland under the English

Parliament. In 1743 he led his congregation at Middle Octorara, Pennsylvania, in a solemn ceremony, crossing swords in celebration of "King Jesus," while condemning the British monarchy. In response, Craighead's presbytery condemned his views and acts as full of "treason, sedition, and distraction," and Craighead removed himself from the presbytery. Moving south, he carried his devotion to the covenants to Virginia and then to the Carolinas. This act to perpetuate the Old World divisions illustrates that some immigrants may have been devoted to "Christ's Kingdom" in America but not committed unanimously to the British kingdom and empire. Such contentiousness grew after the war with France. Reunited Presbyterians and others in the Reformed tradition faced the tensions of the Stamp Act Crisis of 1763 and the era of the American Revolution.

6

Revolution and Constitutions: Civil and Ecclesiastical

During the American Revolution, Horace Walpole said on the floor of the British Parliament that "Cousin America has eloped with a Presbyterian parson." That parson was Scottish immigrant John Witherspoon. A detractor called him "Dr. Silverspoon," a "political drunkard" and a "preacher of sedition." On another occasion, a British soldier described the conflict by saying that it was nothing more than an "Irish-Scotch Presbyterian rebellion."

These judgments are only partly correct. Just after the end of the French and Indian War on the American frontier, the British found themselves embroiled in the tax controversy with the colonies, a tax which was imposed to help pay for the war. The colonists argued for the right of representation in such matters. This controversy led to revolution, beginning in 1775, and also to the writing of America's original political covenants—the Declaration of Independence and the Constitution of the United States of America. Presbyterians constituted only a part of the Reformed family of denominations that dominated American colonial life at the time—Anglicans, Congregationalists, Dutch and German Reformed, and Baptists. Presbyterians were, however, an important part of that tradition in America. These denominations contributed to the revolutionary cause and participated in the shaping of these covenants. Presbyterians played a large role in the conflict, after which they, along with other denominations, organized nationally under new ecclesiastical constitutions. They were influenced by the "contagions of liberty" of this era.

Impending Crisis

For decades, the American colonists had been growing more and more in number, wealth, and independence. Some, such as the Scotch-Irish and a few Scots, lost no love on the mother country. The Stamp Act Crisis of the early 1760s was just one aggravation. The British did not think it was an imposition on the colonists to ask them to help pay the war debt. But it was the principle of taxation without representation that stirred the Boston Tea Party and the tea boycott. Americans wanted representation, some independence. Even nine-year-old Susan Boudinot, the daughter of Presbyterian patriot Elias Boudinot, protested. On a visit to the Tory Governor of New Jersey, who favored the king of England, she was served a cup of tea. She raised it to her lips, but then tossed the contents out the window. After the British relented (for a time), the Presbyterian Synod circulated a pastoral letter giving thanks to God for "English liberties" as well as for the moderate behavior of the king and Parliament as they backed away from this confrontation. The synod called for due submission of citizens to proper authority, along with the celebration of "liberty, civil and religious," without "licentiousness." While this crisis passed, the British began to tighten their control over the colonies with a number of acts that Americans believed oppressive.

The Reverend John Witherspoon (1723–1794) immigrated from Scotland, arriving with his wife Elizabeth in Philadelphia in 1768. A Presbyterian minister, Witherspoon has been involved in a number of controversies over lax doctrine among Scottish ministers, and the control of the Scottish Church by powerful patrons. These ministers and patrons were called "Moderates," who had abandoned the *Westminster Confession* and had adopted much of the nature-creed of the Enlightenment. Witherspoon's satiric attacks, along with other writings, prompted America's New Side Presbyterians to invite him to be president and professor of moral philosophy at the College of New Jersey in Princeton. On his arrival with Elizabeth, he was almost immediately embroiled in politics. He was a Whig who stood for a representative system of government. He began to teach moral philosophy to prospective clergy and civic leaders, including James Madison of Virginia. He also became a member of a group of dissenters, who, following William Livingston and his friends, monitored and opposed all plans to consecrate an Anglican bishop for the colonies. This group of Presbyterians, Congregationalists, and others did not reject the episcopal office so much as they objected to what it had become. They opposed the accumulated economic and political powers and prerogatives of the Anglican establishment. Episcopal power stirred anxiety among some colonial dissenters. They made their concerns known to other dissenters in London who lobbied for their cause. No bishop was consecrated for America until after the Revolution.

Other Presbyterians who had come from Ireland and Scotland found themselves in difficult positions. They joined other colonists to protest colonial rule. Many new immigrants found themselves on America's frontiers, facing hardships, often without the benefit of clergy or the help of civil authorities. They were expected to tame the wilderness and ward off attacks of the Indians on the more settled areas of the country. In western Pennsylvania, this led to the infamous murder of some Moravian Indians by the "Paxton Boys," who felt that the Indians were a threat. In North Carolina, the "Regulators" in the west felt exploited by unscrupulous government officials from the east. In New York, where the British began to billet troops in colonial homes, the "Liberty Boys" rose up against such intimidation. Alexander McDougall, a Scottish immigrant and one of the "Liberty Boys," spent eleven weeks in jail in New York and while behind bars continued his protest against what he considered tyrannical acts. Not all Presbyterians approved of these acts of resistance, preferring other means to deal with the tensions of these years.

Finally, soldiers and citizens shed blood at Lexington and Concord in Massachusetts, and Americans and the British became involved in a civil war. In 1775, the Synod of New York and Philadelphia sent another pastoral letter to constituents, deploring the war, urging continued allegiance to George III, at this point, and cautioning against further inflaming of the public mind. At the same time, the synod reminded Presbyterians of revolutionary principles of their English heritage, of the rights that belonged to all British citizens, and to the legitimacy of the Continental Congress, which by then was assembled in Philadelphia. The synod approved Presbyterian resort to arms on just and necessary occasions. They encouraged a halt to fighting, when the necessity passed. The synod also called for prayer and fasting for peace. Witherspoon, now a representative in Congress from New Jersey, preached a sermon on Psalm 76:10 titled "The Dominion of Providence over the Passion of Men" (1776). He expressed his belief that God might bring some good out of this manifestation of sin in the breakdown of human relations. McDougall became a general in George Washington's army.

Independence and
Political Constitutions

Many Americans, including many Presbyterians, supported American independence and the revolution. Eleven Presbyterians in the Continental Congress—among whom included physician Benjamin Rush, lawyer James Wilson, as well as clergyman Witherspoon—helped shape and then voted for Jefferson's Declaration of Independence of 1776.

The Declaration was, as it has been put, an ex post facto justification of a separation, which John Adams claimed began in the hearts of Americans many years before the 1760s and 1770s. The document, as amended in committee and in Congress, included references to God the Creator, Provider, Judge, the source of nature and nature's laws. It asserted that all human beings are "created equal" and endowed by God with certain inalienable rights, among them "life, liberty and the pursuit of happiness." It also asserted that just governments derive their authority and powers from the "consent of the governed." Although government should not be overthrown lightly, the people had a right to change government when it did not provide for their "safety and happiness." Other members of the Reformed family signed this document.

But not all Presbyterians supported the Declaration. William Smith of New York and John Zubly, a Swiss Reformed minister of Georgia, believed that colonists suffered wrongs but that these wrongs did not warrant rebellion and independence. So did members of the Shippen family in Philadelphia. Meanwhile, a Tory wag attacked Presbyterian revolutionaries, including Witherspoon:

> Member of Congress we must hail him next:
> Come out of Babylon, was now his text.
> Fierce as the fiercest, foremost of the first,
> He'd rail at Kings, with venom well-nigh burst:
>
> Whilst to myself I've humm'd, in dismal tune
> I'd rather be a dog than Witherspoon.
> Be patient, reader—for the issue trust,
> His day will come—remember, Heav'n is just.

Presbyterians served in the army as officers, soldiers, and chaplains. Some had prices put on their heads, as in the case of the Reverends David Caldwell of North Carolina and James Caldwell of New Jersey.

For Presbyterians, the revolution was not an end in itself. They participated in the Congress and then in the formation of the Confederation, and in writing of state and national constitutions. Charles Thomson was Secretary of the Continental Congress and, under the Articles of Confederation, Elias Boudinot served as the first president of the United States, while Ebenezer Hazard became postmaster and the first archivist of the new nation. Presbyterians also took part in writing state constitutions such as those of New Jersey, Pennsylvania, and North Carolina. In Pennsylvania, some supported a unicameral legislature in the belief that human sinfulness in political life is best checked by the people without an upper house. Most Presbyterians, as Whigs, showed their suspicion not only of the power of kings but also the power of the people. They supported bicameral legislatures as another way to prevent political corruption. After the war, the Presbytery of the Eastward in New England wrote about the lack of piety and about sexual misconduct and other sinful behavior aggravated by the war. They warned of God's judgment against the new nation in the midst of celebration. What was true of New England was true of other parts of the country after 1782. Americans turned to the Bible for help. Robert Aitken, a Scottish immigrant, printed the first "purely American" Bible published in English in the United States. It was printed on American paper and was commended by Congress.

Americans considered several proposals for a more effective national government. Finally, in 1787–1788 the Constitutional Convention proposed, and the states approved after extensive debate, the Constitution of the United States of America. Its purpose is stated in the Preamble, which reads:

> We the People of the United States, in order to form a more perfect Union, establish Justice, insure domestic Tranquility, provide for the common Defense, promote the general Welfare, and secure the Blessing of Liberty to ourselves and our posterity, do ordain and establish this Constitution.

All who took office under this Constitution vowed to uphold all the goals of this preamble. Ten, and perhaps eleven, Presbyterian laymen helped shape this document at the Constitutional Convention. Some in the past have argued that the government was modeled after the Presbyterian system of government. It would be more accurate to say that Reformed views of God's sovereignty and of human sinfulness and potential moved those in the new nation to proceed in this direction. While human needs and potential make society necessary and possible, human sinfulness makes it imperative to provide the proper checks and balances and the proper separation, as well as relationships between governmental functions, to keep authority and power from becoming absolute, arbitrary, and corrupt. Witherspoon, as well as Francis Alison (1705–1779) in Philadelphia, lectured on these themes in their moral philosophy courses. James Madison, an Anglican and Witherspoon's student, made a major contribution to the new form of government and defended it in his contribution to the *Federalist Papers*. A few Presbyterians opposed the Constitution in state-ratifying conventions as anti-Federalists, but others voted for it and served under it.

Ecclesiastical Constitutions

As in the case of civil life, religious affairs were also in disarray after the war in the 1780s. Independence called for adjustments, and various Christian denominations began to reorganize structures. Two Scottish Seceder and Covenanter groups, the Associate Presbytery (formed in 1753) and the Reformed Presbytery (formed in 1774), united in 1782 to become the Associate Reformed Synod. Those who did not enter this union continued on as the Associate Synod of North America. These small bodies had to sever their ties to churches in Scotland, a process that caused some tension among their members. The Synod of New York and Philadelphia, however, had no formal ties to churches in the Old World. Many members of the synod were not able to attend meetings during and after the war. Thus they neglected the oversight and the welfare of the whole church. Against this background, the synod met in Philadelphia to form the General Assembly of the Presbyterian Church in the United States of America (PCUSA).

The synod and presbyteries adopted a Constitution for the denomination, including provisions for public worship, doctrinal standards, and the government and discipline of ministers and members. Presbyterians adopted a new American *Directory for the Worship of God.* The denomination had been using the *Directory* of the 1640s. The synod (1) reaffirmed the Presbyterian commitment to both form and freedom in worship; (2) urged Presbyterians to keep Sunday "holy to the Lord"; (3) invited members to gather for worship and to abstain while worshiping from "all whisperings, from salutations, of persons present, of persons coming in, and from gazing about, sleeping, smiling, and all other indecent behavior"; (4) called for a balance of prayer and praise with the preaching of sermons that were well prepared, not too long, and not "public harangues"; (5) provided for the celebration of the Lord's Supper "frequently," with the times to be determined by the minister and the elders; (6) encouraged private and family prayer led by the heads of family, who were admonished to instruct children in the "principles of religion"; and (7) allowed for the singing of hymns by Isaac Watts, and not just the Psalms. This ruling on hymn singing caused a small division in Kentucky, however, because some viewed it as a betrayal of the Scottish psalm-singing tradition. The synod made its ruling to improve congregational singing as a dynamic aspect of worship.

The Constitution also provided for the subscription to the *Westminster Confession* and *Larger* and *Shorter Catechisms*, which contained the "necessary and essential" articles of Christian faith and life, and the "system of doctrine taught in Holy Scriptures." Following, but clarifying the Adopting Act of 1729, presbyteries were allowed to determine, during examination of candidates for the ministry, whether any differences a person might have with the standards placed him outside boundaries of the denomination's standards. As in the past, the denomination attempted to establish parameters but allowed some freedom of conscience in interpreting the doctrine of the church. At last the denomination amended the confession to express an action having to do with the civil magistrate, which was taken in 1729 at the synod meeting. The new paragraphs that were added asserted the church's right to be free from governmental interference, while at the same time insisting on protection from the state in the worship of God according to the dictates of conscience. At the same time, the synod left in the confession the warning that the church should not "intermeddle" in politics, except in "cases extraordinary" and "for the sake of conscience" as allowed by the confession or requested to do so by the civil authorities. The synod also removed from the confession the admonition that Presbyterians were not to tolerate "false religion." This made Presbyterians officially more inclusive than they had been in the past, and it helped them get along better with Roman Catholics. For example, Baltimore clergyman Patrick Allison enjoyed cordial relations with John Carroll, America's first Roman Catholic bishop. Thus Presbyterians adjusted to the new religious and political situation and clarified their ideas in various ways.

The synod produced another document for the Constitution, *The Form of Government and Discipline*, together with *Forms of Process in the Judicatories of this Church*. This document provided rules for the common life of the church. The synod first laid down for the public "general principles" of Presbyterian governance. "God alone," the synod confessed, "is Lord of Conscience" in ecclesiastical as well as political matters. It also declared that "Truth is in order to goodness," that ecclesiastical pronouncements are only "ministerial and declarative," that they should conform to the mind of Christ, and that they should carry no impairment of civil rights. Moreover, Presbyterians wanted no support for their denomination's life from the civil magistrate except that which might be provided for all other denominations. These principles are still part of the church's Constitution. Governing provisions also involved a representative system of clergy and laity who served governing bodies involving congregations, presbyteries, synods, and a General Assembly. Considerable authority and power were located in the presbyteries, though responsibility for review and the welfare of the whole system were placed with the General Assembly. The synod affirmed the right of congregations to choose clerical and lay leaders, although the rules for the elections of elders and deacons were not yet fixed at that time. Presbyteries had the authority and power to examine and ordain and install ministers within congregations.

Congregants were charged with the responsibilities of attending worship and supporting with financial resources the work of the church. The pastor should expect "competent worldly maintenance." Whereas Presbyterian clergy had lived on the contributions of members throughout the colonial period, this provision was an important step in regularizing voluntary support. Some had a hard time getting used to this way of supporting the work of the denomination. "Father" David Rice, responsible for planting Presbyterianism in Kentucky, had an experience that indicated the uncertainties of the ministerial profession. Apparently, for some reason his congregation in Danville cut off his salary. So he refused to administer the Sacrament of Communion. A poet composed a bit of doggerel "On PARSON R__E, Who refused to Perform Divine Service till his arrears were Paid."

> Ye fools! I told you once or twice,
> You'd hear not more from canting R__e;
> He cannot settle his affairs,
> Nor pay attention unto pray'rs,
> Unless you pay up your arrears.
> O how he would in pulpit storm,
> And fill all hell with dire alarm!
> Vengeance pronounce against each vice,
> And, more than all, curs'd avarice;
> Preach'd money was the root of ill,
> Consign'd each rich man until hell;
> But since he finds you will not pay,
> Both rich and poor may go that way.
> 'Tis no more than I expected—
> The meeting-house is now neglected;
> All trades are subject to this chance,
> No longer pipe, no longer dance.

Some church leaders thought that the synod plan sounded too much like a "Scotch hierarchy," which they did not like. Whereas the Scottish model may have been in the minds of some, the General Assembly of the PCUSA was organized from the bottom up. Some suspicious Presbyterians wanted to protect presbytery authority and power. Nevertheless, presbyteries did adopt this Constitution and, in the process, preserved what was called the "seamless coat of Christ"—the unity of the church. The General Assembly was voted into existence in 1788 and held its first meeting in 1789. In 1788 Jedediah Chapman, moderator of the last meeting of the Synod of New York and Philadelphia that debated the new Constitution, preached from the text Eph. 4:3–4, urging Presbyterians to "keep the unity of the Spirit in the bond of peace" (KJV). In 1789, John Witherspoon convened the meeting of the General Assembly and preached a sermon in 1 Cor. 3:7: "So then neither is he that planteth any thing, neither he that watereth; but God that giveth the increase" (KJV). John Rodgers (1727–1811) of the First Presbyterian Church of New York was elected the first moderator of the General Assembly. The minutes of the assembly report 177 ministers, 111 probationers, 215 congregations with ministers, and 205 vacant congregations. The General Assembly carried on ecumenical correspondence and cooperation with other Reformed bodies that were also organizing at the time. It also sent a message of congratulation to George Washington, who was inaugurated president the same year.

The Contagion of Liberty

Along with other Americans, Presbyterians were influenced by what has been called the "contagion of liberty" of this period. The freedoms and rights of women seemed completely neglected by these political and ecclesiastical processes, although some Presbyterians were aware of and reading Mary Wollstonecraft's *Vindication of the Rights of Woman* (1792). The English woman's sexual immorality and religious nonconformity kept them from hearing and adopting her message about women. In the meantime, a Scottish widow, Isabella Graham, encouraged by Witherspoon, immigrated to New York in 1789 and established a girl's school, which soon had fifty pupils. She also joined others in founding charitable institutions, including the Society for the Relief of Poor Widows with Small Children.

Presbyterians could not avoid dealing with religious liberty. So influential had Presbyterians become that in 1781 the synod had to reassure the public about its intentions: "The Synod do solemnly and publicly declare that they ever have and still do, renounce and abhor the principles of intolerance, and we do believe that every peaceable member of civil society ought to be protected in the full and free exercise of religion." The Presbytery of Hanover, following ideas of Davies, supported the enactment of Jefferson's "Act for Religious Liberty" in Virginia in 1786 with several thoughtful petitions—memorials—that were addressed to the legislature. This support for religious liberty, going back to Makemie's trial in New York over his encounter with Lord Cornbury, helped create the ethos for the passage of the First Amendment to the Constitution in 1791: "Congress shall make no law respecting an establishment of religion or prohibiting the free exercise thereof. . . ." The religious clauses were linked with provisions for civil liberties, including freedom of speech, of the press, of peaceable assembly, and of the right to petition Congress for a redress of grievances. Some Presbyterians were concerned about the emergence of "anythingarians" and "nothingarians" in the society, but in general they supported the move to voluntarism. This reversed fifteen hundred years of Constantianism in the era of Christian history. It was concluded that coercion in religious matters made mean and hypocritical people, and that voluntarism was healthier for both religious and civil institutions.

Presbyterians also faced the issue of slavery. Some sensed and publicly deplored the hypocrisy of the revolutionary rhetoric of freedom while, at the same time, Americans denied freedom to a whole class of people— African Americans. Slavery persisted as an institution in the new nation. Neither in the Declaration of Independence nor the Constitution to which Presbyterians agreed addressed this issue justly or consistently. However, in 1787, the Presbyterian Synod of New York and Philadelphia issued a public pronouncement. God made "of one flesh all the children of men," and made us all a part of one family. Slavery was condemned on biblical, Christian, and humanitarian grounds. The synod called on members to instruct slaves and to work for emancipation at a "moderate rate" so that African Americans might be freed and participate in the "privileges of civil society." Some Presbyterians—for example, layman Joseph Bryan of Philadelphia—helped organize some of the earliest antislavery societies.

Native Americans were treated as foreigners in their own land and as subjects to be Christianized and civilized by missionaries in the church. Native American Samson Occum lived through the American Revolution. He noted in the political rhetoric of the times the references to America as a promised land. Yet he and his Mohegan people were being forced to move westward because of new European immigrants and American hunger for more space. Occum somewhat mournfully joined his people to offer them the comforts of the Gospel. Some Presbyterians expressed millennialist expectations. A young New England clergyman, David Austin, while pastor of the Elizabethtown, New Jersey, Presbyterian Church, believed in the imminent return of Jesus. He was pastor of such eminent leaders as Elias Boudinot and William Livingston. After studying

Daniel and Revelation and reflecting on the revolutions, spiritual and political, of the 1740s, 1770s, and 1780s, he predicted that Christ would
come in 1796. His prophecy failed, the congregation finally asked the
presbytery to dissolve the pastoral relationship.

More cautious Presbyterians held that Jesus would come in "due time."
Meanwhile, Presbyterians who participated in the shaping of the new nation continued to do so by obeying what Presbyterian poet Sidney Lanier
refers to as the "Onward ache" to the West. They sought ways of nurturing faith and life and ways to face the problems of the new and expanding nation.

7

Revivals, Voluntarism, and "Freedom's Ferment"

With the deaths of John Witherspoon in 1794 and of George Washington in 1799, a decisive era in American history ended, and, according to one author, an era of "freedom's ferment" began for the new nation. It was also a new era for the Presbyterian Church in the United States of America (PCUSA). Immigrants began to flow once again from the British Isles and the continent, and Americans pressed westward across the Ohio, Cumberland, and Mississippi Rivers into the Northwest Territory and the Louisiana Purchase. Americans carved new states out of this land. They used the trails, rivers, canals, and, eventually, the railroads, which tied the nation together. Philadelphian Presbyterian Matthias W. Baldwin pioneered in the locomotive building that revolutionized travel and aided the settlement of the West. Presbyterians began to expand the American enterprise globally. Clipper ships carried American goods to the world and brought the world's goods to America. In the War of 1812 the British humiliated the Yankees, until Andrew "Old Hickory" Jackson won the Battle of New Orleans. He was elected the first president of the nation with Presbyterian affiliation. He rode out of Tennessee to Washington, D.C., to offer a less deferential, more democratic style, which was troublesome to some Presbyterians and also to other people. Americans, according to some, were fulfilling the "manifest destiny" or, as one clergy put it, "providential destiny" of the United States and of the Christian community.

Robert Baird, a Presbyterian missionary to Roman Catholics in Europe, captured the spirit of the age in a book titled *Religion in America,* first published in 1843. Baird described major denominations who traced their beginnings to the European Reformation, and who had been organized for the most part at the time of the American Revolution. He called these bodies evangelical, excluding Catholics and Unitarians. Although preserving

European practices, adherents of these traditions also held revivals and organized numerous voluntary societies through which individuals from these various denominations sought to influence the nation and the world. They built educational institutions, carried on home and world missions, and tried to reform the nation. Presbyterians were deeply involved in these developments, which touched all aspects of Presbyterian faith and life.

Church Planting, Revivals, and "Freedom's Ferment"

As Presbyterians pressed westward with other Americans, they organized new congregations wherever they went. David Rice formed a church for Transylvania Presbytery in Kentucky. The congregants gathered in 1790 under the following principles:

1. A church is a society of Christians, voluntarily associated together, for the worship of God, and spiritual improvement and usefulness.
2. A visible church consists of visible or apparent Christians.
3. The children of visible Christians are members of the visible church, though in a state of minority.
4. A visible Christian is one who understands the doctrines of the Christian religion, is acquainted with a work of God's Spirit in effectual calling, professes repentance from dead works, and faith in our Lord Jesus Christ, and subjection to him as a king; and whose life and conversation correspond to his profession.
5. Sealing ordinances ought not to be administered to such as are not visible Christians.
6. A charitable allowance ought to be made for such, whose natural abilities are weak, or who have not enjoyed good opportunities of religious instruction, when they appear to be humble and sincere.
7. Children and youth descended from church members, though not admitted to all the privileges of the church, are entitled to the instructions of the church and subjected to its discipline.

Presbyterians organized numerous congregations under these and other principles during those years. For various reasons, such as requiring high standards for training ministers and for ordination, Presbyterians lost out numerically to the Methodists and the Baptists in the planting of churches in some areas. As did adherents of these denominations, Presbyterians carried on revivals in which they ascertained the work of God's Spirit and brought people into the churches. Baird wrote that revivals were so prevalent that the historian could not easily trace them.

Some of these revivals occurred on college campuses, where heart stirrings were wedded to the pursuit of knowledge. After the American Revolution, some college students expressed disdain for Christian faith and life and championed the Deist ideas of persons such as Tom Paine. At the newly formed Hampden-Sydney College in Virginia, named after English revolutionaries, some students boasted of their infidelity, while others experienced conversion and began to meet secretly in their rooms for prayer and singing. They were harassed by their colleagues. President John Blair Smith (1756–1799) intervened. He protected and encouraged them on their Christian pilgrimage. Yale students showed the same hostility to religion, calling one another by the names of infamous continental infidels such as Voltaire, as they entered the chapel for worship. President Timothy Dwight (1752–1817) met this kind of impiety with vigorous intellectual arguments and caused a revival at Yale among his students. He wrote and taught students to sing "I Love Thy Kingdom, Lord." At the College of New Jersey, student life was also marred by irreverence, which sometimes degenerated into riots. When Ashbel Green assumed the presidency in 1812, he delivered an inaugural address titled "The Union of Piety and Science," indicating the marriage of Christian piety and the life of the mind. Similarly, some Princeton students experienced a deepening of their convictions. These revivals produced numerous dedicated and disciplined ministers and laity for leadership in the church and society.

Meanwhile, revivals of a different character were taking place on the American frontier. Some Presbyterians such as the Reverend James McGready took the leadership of these awakenings, especially those at Cane Ridge, Kentucky. McGready's heart had been warmed by the revival at Hampden-Sydney College. According to reports, thousands of people gathered at camp meetings, pitched their tents, and for days attended religious services conducted by clergy of various denominations. At night, the flickering light from the candles, lanterns, and campfires made the gatherings awesome experiences. One participant estimated that twenty thousand people attended one revival where preachers addressed the emotions more than the understanding. The heavens were rent, he wrote, as people cried for God's mercy with "shrieks and shouts." They were convulsed with dancing and the "jerks," as they were called. Some Presbyterians, including McGready, recoiled from this kind of revival, which seemed to address the emotions rather than the understanding, and preferred a moderate expression of piety that became prevalent among Presbyterians. These gatherings may have reminded recent immigrants from Scotland and Ireland of Communion Seasons held in the Old World, which were also large social as well as religious events. They may have made people feel more at home in their isolated existence on the American frontier.

Charles Grandison Finney (1792–1875), a New York lawyer turned preacher, became the symbol of revivalism in this era of "freedom's ferment." After a vivid conversion experience of his own, he associated with a Presbyterian Church under the influence of his pastor. He held revivals in cities, in towns, and in the country, drawing larger and larger crowds with his personal and anecdotal preaching. He felt he could not accept aspects of the *Westminster Confession,* so was drawn toward the more moderate Presbyterians and Congregationalists. In 1835 he delivered *Lectures on Revivals of Religion,* which were widely read and very influential. He analyzed revival experiences in terms of using means to obtain results. The use of means, or "new measures," such as protracted meetings, anxious meetings, and anxious benches guaranteed conversions. Some Presbyterians opposed Finney because of this emphasis on means over substance, thus compromising conversion, interpreted by Edwards and Davies as a work of God's grace alone. Finney was called to be the pastor of the Free Presbyterian Church (that is, free from pews rents) in New York. He later became professor and president at Oberlin College, which was the first American institution to admit women and African Americans. He preached widely throughout America and the British Isles and extended his influence through his published lectures. Other Presbyterians, such as Daniel Baker in the South, adapted Finney's approach but stressed the divine aspect of the work of redemption.

Frontier Cooperation and Division

Whereas revivals represented a very personal aspect of Presbyterian faith and life, Presbyterians also engaged in building congregations on the frontier along the lines set down by David Rice's congregation. In this way, they emphasized the corporate character of the Christian experience. Presbyterians organized congregations, baptized children, and disciplined members for immorality. As in the colonial period, churches continued to serve as the first moral courts on the frontier prior to the organization of civil authority. When they had gathered enough congregations, Presbyterians organized presbyteries and synods, thus emphasizing the connectional nature of the Reformed tradition. In the era of "freedom's ferment," tensions often arose between the American individualism and corporate responsibility for the whole, which Presbyterians considered essential to a faithful Christian life.

Populations flowed into western New York, Ohio, Indiana, Illinois, Kentucky, Tennessee, Alabama, Mississippi, Louisiana, and Texas. Moving into these new states, Presbyterians cooperated with Congregationalists in planting congregations. They did so through a Plan of Union agreed to in 1801. The Plan was intended to curb the competition for members between the churches. But the two communions had to deal with the differences in church governance. In an ecumenical spirit, congregations were allowed to call either a Presbyterian or Congregational pastor. When conflict arose, they could appeal to either Presbyterian or Congregational governing bodies in a given situation, or to a council made up of an equal number of both denominations. The congregation could be represented in a presbytery by elders or in an association by elders or congregational committee members. A sincere attempt to cooperate, the plan was approved by the General Assembly of the PCUSA and the Congregational Association of Connecticut. Participants in the plan were dubbed Presbygationalists. Congregationalists had not as yet organized a national denomination; some were therefore lukewarm to this enterprise. Tensions arose among those Presbyterians who believed the plan compromised confessional commitments and structures. Both denominations also cooperated with one another through the American Home Missionary Society founded in New York in 1826.

Some Presbyterians parted company with the General Assembly, founding the Disciples of Christ, and the Cumberland Presbyterian Church in 1810. The Kentucky revival experiences prompted some Presbyterians to emphasize a restoration of a true New Testament church without the accretions of eighteen hundred years of tradition. Under the Reverend Alexander Campbell, a Scottish Presbyterian, those persons called themselves Disciples of Christ, as they attempted to restore a New Testament church. Where the Bible spoke, they claimed, they spoke; where the Bible is silent, they were silent. Other Presbyterians in the Cumberland region wanted to engage in what they thought was a more effective ministry on the western frontier. Deeply affected by the revival experiences in Kentucky, they questioned some aspects of the *Westminster Confession*. They thought that the doctrine of election was too fatalistic. They also questioned the standards of the denomination for the ordination of clergy as too restrictive. In this latter case, the Transylvania and Cumberland presbyteries ordained deeply religious but formally uneducated persons to the ministry to exhort and catechize, contrary to Presbyterian order. The Synod of Kentucky censored the presbyteries for ordaining Finis Ewing. In response, Samuel M'Adoo, Samuel King, and Ewing met in Dickson, Tennessee, and constituted a presbytery in 1810. This grew into the Cumberland Presbyterian Church (CPC). Although this new denomination was willing to waive requirements for formal education, in some cases, it did not abandon all educational requirements. It founded educational institutions. The CPC reaffirmed the *Westminster Confession* but restated the doctrine of predestination in order to express divine love for all God's children. The denomination expanded in the South and Southwest. In 1837, The Reverend Sumner Bacon took the lead in organizing the first CPC presbytery in Texas. Although it is difficult to find accurate statistics for the earliest development of the CPC, reports from eighteen of thirty-five presbyteries in 1835 account for 167 ministers, 243 congregations, and 17,719 communicants.

The PCUSA attempted to prevent this division but failed. In fact, instead of adapting educational standards to special situations, the denomination expanded its criteria for ordination to the ministry. Although it engaged in considerable theological debate, the PCUSA denomination did not revise its confessional standards at that time. These stances contributed to the larger numerical growth of denominations such as the Baptists and the Methodists rather than the Presbyterians in the era. Moreover, worried about what seemed like unbridled democratic ferment, the denomination began to debate the office of the elder and then to define it more clearly. Some wished to emphasize the importance of the lay office in order to ensure the benefits of a representative system of government for the whole church and the society. The Reverend Samuel Miller, a noted New York pastor, wrote an *Essay on the Warrant, Nature, and Duties of the Office of the Ruling Elder in the Presbyterian Church* (1831). He argued for an eldership that would, by implication, help prevent the growth of a clerical caste in America, on the one hand, and prevent the danger of unbridled democracy that would undermine the nation as well as the church, on the other. He described his proposals as a "Presbyterian Republicanism" that would provide the checks and balances essential for any healthy community.

Educational and Missionary Endeavors

During those early years of the nineteenth century, Presbyterians helped shape a "benevolent empire" of voluntary societies, which existed alongside denominational structures. These societies drew together individuals who wanted to encourage educational, missionary, and reforming work among Christians. Presbyterians in pursuing this strategy cooperated with other Reformed communions and Christians across denominational lines. Many Presbyterians began to realize that some of these functions were corporate in nature and required the response of all Presbyterians, not simply those who were drawn for personal reasons to special causes.

When the Reverend Lyman Beecher (1775–1863), a Presbygationalist from New England, became head of Lane Theological Seminary in Cincinnati, he wrote a *Plea for the West* (1835). In it he called on Christians to educate, educate, educate and to make the nation a better place, especially the West. Beecher thought the Reformed churches were losing the battle for American hearts and minds, so Presbyterians helped organize and support educational work at all levels. They then championed the American Bible Society (1816) and the American Tract Society (1824), and "colporteurs" distributed Bibles, books, and pamphlets on their travels north, south, east, and west. Similarly, persons such as Alexander Henry of Philadelphia, along with Joanna Bethune (1770–1860) of New York, encouraged the education of children. Bethune, daughter of Isabella Graham, helped organize the American Sunday School Union in 1824, and soon became known as the "mother of the Sabbath School in America." Bethune wrote of her relationship to Christ and her motivation for performing educational and the charitable work. While attending the worship one Sunday, she felt pensive and lonely until the minister read the words of John 20:16: "Jesus saith unto her, Mary. She turned herself and saith unto him, Rabboni; which is to say, Master" (KJV). Bethune describes her reaction: "When the pastor read the verse, and paused on the word 'Mary,' it went to my heart, and I could not help claiming my Saviour as much as if he at that moment said, 'Joanna': and in the sweet confidence of faith my heart responded, 'Rabboni, Master!'" She continues: "However discouraged at the difficulties I have had to encounter, both public and private, a feeling that my Redeemer cared for me, and that the Lord Himself upheld me with His arm, has sustained me."

During these years, Presbyterians, with some caution, began to adopt and adapt the Sunday school as an aspect of the work of a Board of Education. The Sunday school contributed to the expansion of the public school, which Presbyterians in general supported. Presbyterian William McGuffey (1800–1873), educator and professor of moral philosophy, first in Ohio and then at the University of Virginia, produced in his *Eclectic Reader* (1836). His various *Readers* helped shape the habits of virtue among America's children.

Presbyterians, along with Congregationalists, intensified activity in the field of higher education energetically, with a mixture of strategies. Presbyterians also organized numerous residential colleges in the nineteenth century, including Davidson College in North Carolina, Centre College in Kentucky, Lafayette College in Pennsylvania, Muskingum College in Ohio, Illinois College, and many others. With Congregationalists, they organized so many colleges that it has been said that church education was American higher education. But Presbyterians also invested much energy in the development of the Universities of North Carolina, Georgia, Tennessee, Ohio, Michigan, and later the University of California, among others. These institutions promoted higher education for all citizens. Presbyterians also began to realize that there was no essential difference between the intellectual capacities of females and males. William Sprague, a minister, suggested that Presbyterians ought to provide higher education as "reparations" to women who had been wronged by being denied such an opportunity. So Presbyterians also organized women's colleges, among them Mary Baldwin in Virginia, Agnes Scott in Georgia, and Lindenwood College in Missouri. Presbyterian clergy who often presided over these institutions taught courses in moral philosophy to encourage responsible Christian living. Joseph Henry, a Presbyterian and professor of science at the College of New Jersey, became the nation's educator as head of the newly born Smithsonian Institution in Washington, D.C.

During the latter part of the eighteenth and early nineteenth centuries, as a denomination the PCUSA decided that the apprenticeship approach to theological education was not completely satisfactory. Presbyterians in western Pennsylvania first started a school for educating ministers at Service Seminary in 1794. The denomination then organized a Theological Seminary at Princeton in 1812, under the leadership of the Reverend Archibald Alexander. Alexander, who had been influenced by the Virginia revivals, became the pastor of the Pine Street Presbyterian Church. He was then called to Princeton Theological Seminary to be its first professor. Presbyterians also founded Union Theological Seminary in Virginia (1812); Auburn Theological Seminary in Auburn, New York (1818), now a part of Union Theological Seminary in New York (1836); Western Theological Seminary (1827), now a part of Pittsburgh Theological Seminary (1959); Columbia Theological Seminary in South Carolina (1828), now in Decatur, Georgia, and Lane Theological Seminary in Cincinnati (1829), now a part of McCormick Theological Seminary (1830). These institutions were founded to ensure the continuation of a learned as well as a faithful ministry. While all ministerial candidates were expected to have collegiate degrees, the seminaries sometimes distanced themselves from colleges because of a concern for the orthodoxy of college personnel.

Presbyterians expanded global consciousness through mission societies. They had been engaged in evangelical work among Native Americans and African Americans. In the religious ferment of the era they began to send missionaries overseas to fulfill what has been called the "Great Commission" of Christ:

> And Jesus came and said to them, "All authority in heaven and on earth has been given to me. Go therefore and make disciples of all nations, baptizing them in the name of the Father and of the Son and of the Holy Spirit, and teaching them to obey everything that I have commanded you. And remember, I am with you always, to the end of the age." (Matt. 28:18–20)

The enthusiasm of college students, as a matter of fact, motivated Reformed leaders to organize the American Board of Commissioners for Foreign Missions (1810), a voluntary society that drew together Congregationalists, Presbyterians, and Dutch Reformed in the evangelistic enterprise. This Boston-based board raised funds, recruited and consecrated missionaries and their wives, and sent them to work among Native Americans and to the Middle East, India, China, and Africa. Presbyterian merchants such as David Oliphant and Robert Ralston contributed to these efforts by booking passage on their ships for these emissaries of Christ. In fulfilling the "Great Commission," these missionaries found themselves also fulfilling the "Great Commandment of Love" to feed the hungry, satisfy the thirsty, befriend the friendless, clothe the naked, and visit the sick and those in prison. They remembered Christ's words: "Truly I tell you, just as you did it to one of the least of these who are members of my family, you did it to me" (Matt. 25:40).

Presbyterian and Congregational missionaries resisted the attempts of the state of Georgia to appropriate Cherokee land, especially after gold had been discovered on Indian territory. In a court case that found its way to the Supreme Court in the United States, Presbyterian lawyer William Wirt argued and won the case for the Cherokees. But Presbyterian President Andrew Jackson refused to enforce the court decision in the 1830s and proceeded to move the Cherokees on a "Trail of Tears" to Oklahoma. Presbygationalist missionary Samuel Worcester, who defended the Cherokees, was arrested and sentenced to a Georgia prison. Upon his release, he then accompanied the Native Americans on their disastrous journey west.

The PCUSA developed its own mission enterprises as early as 1801. It also cooperated with the American Board of Commissioners for Foreign Missions (ABCFM). Some Presbyterians, including John Holt Rice (1777–1831) of Union Theological Seminary in Virginia, thought missions were so important that all Christians, not simply interested individuals, should be involved in spreading the Gospel. Holt put it this way: "The Presbyterian Church in the United States is a missionary society, the object of which is to aid in the conversion of the world, and every member of the church is a member for life of said society, and bound in maintenance of his Christian character, to do all in his power for the accomplishment of the object." Presbyterians gradually expanded their own foreign and home boards to fulfill Rice's vision of the denomination as a whole, supporting this mission work.

Reforming America

In this period of "freedom's ferment," Presbyterians also joined in organizing voluntary societies to improve the morality of the nation. Ezra Stiles Ely, a former Stated Clerk and moderator of the General Assembly, attempted to deal with reform in a very different way. In his sermon in 1827 titled "The Duty of Christian Freemen to Elect Christian Rulers," he advocated the formation of a "Christian Party" in politics and supported Andrew Jackson for president against the Unitarian, John Quincy Adams. The public, however, did not accept this idea.

Presbyterians, rather, joined other Americans in attempts to do various things in numerous voluntary associations that they thought contributed to the welfare of all peoples. Concerned, for example, about the different approach to the Sabbath of recent immigrants from Europe, they helped form the General Union for Promoting the Observance of the Christian Sabbath, under the leadership of Stephen van Rensselaer. Through this respect for Sunday, they wished to witness to a belief that all life belongs to God who creates us and redeems the world. They also joined others in a movement to curb the abuse of alcoholic beverages, to make more sober families, workers, and citizens. Although not all Presbyterians endorsed the total abstinence cause, they did agree on the need for sobriety. Many supported the American Temperance Union formed in 1836.

The War of 1812 stimulated discussion of the use of violence among nations. Presbyterian Alexander McLeod wrote a tract defending war on "just and necessary" occasions as taught in the *Westminster Confession*. Other Presbyterians were sick and tired of warfare. Merchant David Low Dodge, a Presbyterian, became a pacifist and helped organize the American Peace Society in 1828. He used to slip peace tracts into packages of goods he shipped from his business to customers. In fact, Americans organized so many reforming societies that one writer mused: A man could not kiss his wife without receiving permission from one of them. Promoters of such societies were accused, by one observer, of "Protestant Jesuitism" because of their ways and means. Impatience for reform increased utopian expectations, and reformers often moved from a position of gradualism to immediatism, moderation to extremism, and voluntarism to coercion.

Slavery, however, persisted as the great moral problem of the age. In 1787 the Synod of New York and Philadelphia condemned slavery. The General Assembly renewed this condemnation over the years, and then again, in a longer statement of 1818, softening their condemnation by including some compromises. This statement carried an admonition to members that they should not use the "plea of necessity" to keep from facing up to and eliminating the evil. The Presbyterians were divided: some supported the American Colonization Society (1817), which proposed to send freed slaves back to Africa to help christianize and civilize Africans; some were abolitionists who supported the American Anti-Slavery Society (1833), whose members favored and campaigned for the immediate liberation of slaves. Some Presbyterians, and others especially in the south, defended slavery and considered it an economic and political problem, not a spiritual one. It fell, therefore, outside the bounds of ecclesiastical discussion and responsibility. These persons sought to keep the issue from being raised at meetings of the governing bodies of the church. Many were emancipationists who recognized the evils of slavery, but hoped for a gradual solution to the problem.

The issue would not disappear, however. A small but articulate group of African-American Presbyterian pastors including John Gloucester, Theodore Wright, and Samuel Cornish (1795–1799), expressed their hostility to slavery in America. Cornish helped publish the first black newspaper, *Freedom's Journal* (1827), the motto of which was "Righteousness exalteth a nation." As the debate grew more intense, the General Assembly could not make any statements about the issue. The tension grew more severe when a mob went after Elijah Lovejoy, a white Presbyterian minister, newspaper editor, and abolitionist. Mobs destroyed his presses in St. Louis and Alton, Illinois, and another mob finally murdered him in Alton, in 1837. Lovejoy became a martyr for the cause of freedom of the press, as well as for the freedom of African Americans.

Old School and New School

In 1837–1838 the PCUSA suffered another split, then known as the Old School–New School division. The separation involved differences over theology, governance, and reform, especially slavery. These issues were related. The Old School was doctrinally more conservative than the New School and had many adherents in the South. New Schoolers were exploring fresh ways of expressing their Reformed theology. Many were located in New York, in the Midwest, and in border states. More deeply involved in the operation of the Plan of Union, they were influenced by liberal shifts in Calvinism in New England. They were attempting to articulate more clearly the human response to God's gracious love shown in Jesus Christ. Despite New School professions of faithfulness to the Reformed faith, Old School adherents, especially in Pennsylvania, suspected a lack of New School orthodoxy. The Old School believed that New School strength came into the General Assembly through the Plan of Union of 1801. This involved Congregationlists, who did not have to subscribe to the *Westminster Confession* or accept the governance and discipline of the Presbyterian Church. Furthermore, some of the New School adherents were abolitionists, many wanting to conform their lives to the denomination's statements about the "peculiar institution." Many southerners of the Old School constituency had begun to defend slavery as a positive good, marred only by ill treatment of slaves.

In 1837, the Old School constituency controlled the General Assembly. In a pre-Assembly meeting, one southerner from Virginia maintained that blood would soon flow in the Potomac if the church did not stop arguing about slavery. During the Assembly, the Old School did several things: (1) abrogated the Plan of Union under which the denomination had operated since 1801; (2) made this action retroactive; and (3) in a political maneuver, excised the Synods of Western Reserve, Utica, Geneva, and Genessee, which were organized under the Plan of Union, making them no longer members of the denomination. Presbyterians in the slaveholding states constituted less than one-eighth of the New School but more than one-third of the Old School. The southerners were threatening to withdraw from the denomination because of agitation over slavery, and some Old School leaders feared becoming a minority, should the southerners carry out this threat. Other Old School leaders were not supporters of slavery and urged a gradualist approach to manumission; however, abolitionists had grown impatient with this position. The Old Schoolers preferred to see the division of the church along theological and governance, rather than sectional, lines. It should be noted that Old Schoolers were developing boards and agencies to deal with denominational responsibilities, thus making cooperation with voluntary societies less necessary.

The Old School considered itself the Reforming Party. It thought this division was the right move because of the theological and governance issues at stake. Those in the South supported the Old School acts of 1837 to gain some relief from antislavery pressures, as well as to show sympathy with other Old School theology. The New Schoolers became known as the Constitutional Party. They believed that the Old School acted contrary to procedures of decency and order under which Presbyterians had lived for more than half a century. In the "Auburn Declaration" of 1837, New School leaders confessed their own commitment to the Presbyterian Church and its "Doctrine, Worship," and "Government." This division illustrates how difficult it was for Presbyterians to seek the peace and unity as well as the purity of the church.

Some people thought that this Old School–New School division was an ominous national event because of the role Presbyterians played in society. Cyrus McCormick, Presbyterian industrialist, considered the PCUSA (Old School) as the only institution holding the country together. Abolitionist William Lloyd Garrison considered the division between the Old School and the Presbyterian Church (New School) a sign of the coming division of the nation, a concern heightened in the 1840s by the division of the Methodists and the Baptists over slavery. The failure of the major evangelical Protestant bodies, including Presbyterians, to resolve the great American dilemma, slavery, had fatal national consequences.

In this same period, however, Thomas Kennedy (1776–1832), a recent Scottish immigrant and a devout Presbyterian, advanced freedom on another front. He was elected in 1817 as a delegate to the Maryland Assembly, where he discovered that the state's constitution discriminated against Jews. Strongly influenced by Thomas Jefferson, he felt the injustice of a law that denied Jews the right to worship God according to the dictates of conscience. He helped to write "An act to extend to the sect of people professing the Jewish religion, the same rights and privileges that are enjoyed by Christians." In arguing for the act he reminded his hearers of the strength of prejudice, especially religious prejudice going back eighteen hundred years. After a long struggle, a bill granting full religious freedom to Jews finally passed the legislature in 1826, largely because of Kennedy's persistence. In connection with this effort, he wrote a poem about his motivation. It reads in part as follows:

> I blush for Christians that they should forget,
> The Golden Rule—their great Law-giver set,
> That they the precious precept should condemn,
> Which their ador'd Redeemer taught to them.
> Do unto others—as you'd wish they'd do
> In the same situation unto you.

Thus, in an age of "freedom's ferment," a layman summoned Christians to faithfulness in all areas of life.

8

Continental Challenges and the Irrepressible Conflict

In 1852, Old School Presbyterians, meeting in General Assembly at Charleston, South Carolina, formed the Presbyterian Historical Society. The denomination had expressed a historical consciousness as early as 1791 when the Stated Clerk began to collect ecclesiastical documents. In Charleston, the Reverend Cortland van Rensselaer, secretary of the Board of Education, declared the society to be "a school of learning, a knowledge-receiving and knowledge-imparting institution." Samuel Agnew, a businessman, served as first librarian and treasurer in Philadelphia, where the organization was located. The society assisted Richard Webster in publishing *The History of the Presbyterian Church* (1857). It is also the oldest continuous denominational historical body in the country.

Such historical consciousness was expressed during a pivotal period of American history. The nation expanded geographically, embracing the Republic of Texas in 1845, and also adding territory taken in the Mexican-American War in 1848. This new territory included New Mexico, Arizona, California, Nevada, and parts of Wyoming, Colorado, and Oklahoma. In 1846, the nation also claimed from Great Britain and finally occupied half of the Oregon Territory. The Gold Rush to California, the rush for other lucrative metals of the Rocky Mountain area, and the farm rush stimulated by the Homestead Act of 1862, accelerated western expansion. America experienced the immigration of approximately 5,500,000 people, many from Catholic Ireland and Germany, and Asia, especially China. These new immigrants helped build the transcontinental railroad that helped to make the country one.

Philip Schaff (1819–1893), a recent immigrant and a member of the German Reformed Church, wrote a seminal book *America*, in 1852. A professor at Mercersburg Theological Seminary, he observed that the

Reformed and Presbyterian churches dominated American life, although they were losing out numerically to the Baptists, Methodists, and Roman Catholics. He also reemphasized that the distinguishing principles of all Protestants were the doctrines of justification by faith and the supremacy of the Scriptures as the rule faith and life. The largest body of Presbyterians, which was divided into the PCUSA (Old School), PCUSA (New School), and others such as the CPC, was joined by the new United Presbyterian Church of North America (UPCNA) in 1858. As Presbyterians moved with the population across the continent, planting churches, they also faced changes in worship, theological emphases, governance, and missions. They also fought on both sides of a bloody Civil War that finally consolidated the nation and led to the abolition of slavery. Although the war divided Presbyterians North and South, it also led to cooperative enterprises and the reunion of the Old School and New School in the North and West during and after the war.

United Presbyterian Church
of North America

A number of Scottish groups immigrated from Scotland during the colonial period and settled in New York, South Carolina, and western Pennsylvania, among other places. After the American Revolution, they organized as Covenanters and Seceders. Some of them were deeply concerned that America's new Constitution did not profess explicitly that Christ is head of the nation. In 1858, two of these denominations, the General Synod of the Associate Reformed Church and the Synod of the Associate Presbyterian Church (Seceders), joined in Pittsburgh, Pennsylvania, to form the United Presbyterian Church of North America (UPCNA). This union included the majority of the heirs of these Scottish traditions. Although pious, the Scots had not yet been influenced much by American revivalism. But the religious ferment of 1857–1858, during the economic depression, deeply impressed the Presbyterians and encouraged the union of churches. The new denomination embraced the *Westminster Confession* and the *Larger* and *Shorter Catechisms*, which had been adopted by Scottish Presbyterians in the seventeenth century. It also accepted a "Judicial Testimony," which stated certain "distinctives" of the church. These included the principle of covenanting with God and one another, the exclusive use of psalms for praise in worship, and the opposition to oath-bound secret societies and to slavery. It also claimed the right to exclude from the Lord's Supper those who did not adhere to the denomination's tenets. According to statistics of 1859, the union brought together a total of 408 ministers, 634 congregations, and 55,547 members—a constituency fervently committed to missions. The church rapidly developed missions, especially in Egypt and other areas of the Middle East. The Associated Reformed Presbyterian Church in the South did not join this ecumenical venture.

Changes in
Christian Faith and Life

The main body of Presbyterians, the PCUSA—both the Old School and New School factions—faced challenges in the burgeoning American society, now on a continental scale. The two schools grew along parallel lines, and this development brought the two bodies closer over the years. The New School did not want the division in the first place, and numerous Old School leaders, for example, those at Princeton Theological Seminary, were opposed to it also. Developments in worship, theology, governance, and missions illustrate continuing tensions and also willingness to work together.

Both Schools continued to live with the *Directory,* trying to preserve both freedom and order in the worship of God. Presbyterian worship tended to be clerically centered and didactic, with an emphasis on the reading and interpretation of the Scriptures. All Presbyterians, however, were influenced by revivals that enlivened the worship life of congregations. The New Schoolers, many of them located in New York, were more under the sway of Charles Finney than were Old Schoolers, who were suspicious of Finney's theology and his stress on means of grace. The Old School had its own popular leaders, such as Daniel Baker, who preached revivals through the South and into Texas. Both Schools were influenced by the revival that started on Fulton Street (New York), with its lay leadership and its prayer meetings, during 1857–1858 and thereafter. A sign seen at one meeting read:

> Prayers & Exhortations
> Not to Exceed 5 minutes,
> in order to give all an opportunity.
> Not more than 2 consecutive
> Prayers or Exhortations.
> No Controverted Points
> Discussed.

Presbyterian women could not speak in church gatherings attended by both men and women, which were referred to as "promiscuous meetings,"

but they made contributions to worship indirectly through writing conversion novels and verses that were sometimes turned into popular
hymns. Susan and Anna Warner, who taught a Sunday school class at
West Point for years, wrote for a livelihood. Susan preached in her widely
read novel *The Wide, Wide World* (1851). Although a critic called it
"fudge," it added to the Warners' popularity. A poem in *Say and Seal*
(1859), another conversion novel, became the most popular hymn of the
Sunday school movement. A Sunday school teacher sings these words to
a dying boy:

> Jesus loves me, this I know,
> For the Bible tells me so;
> Little ones to him belong,
> They are weak but he is strong.

> Jesus loves me—he who died,
> Heaven's gate to open wide;
> He will wash away my sin,
> Let his little child come in.

> Jesus loves me, loves me still,
> Though I'm very weak and ill;
> From this shining throne on high,
> Comes to watch me where I lie.

> Jesus loves me—he will stay
> Close beside me all the way,
> Then his little child will take
> Up to heaven for his dear sake.

Elizabeth Prentiss, wife of a professor at Union Theological Seminary
(N.Y.) wrote "More Love to Thee, O Christ, More Love to Thee!" Her
novel, *Stepping Heavenward* (1869), showed her own talent for preaching
and was read by thousands in America and Europe.

At the same time, Presbyterians, began to rediscover a rich Reformed
heritage in worship. This liturgical revival was stimulated, in part, because Presbyterians became more affluent and built grander churches.
Levi Ward, a Rochester, New York, businessman and an Old School Presbyterian in New School territory, built a handsome Romanesque building
for the congregation with which he worshiped. He composed liturgical

forms and prayers for services, including some for weddings, funerals, and the administration of the sacraments. Clergyman historian, Charles W. Baird gave impetus to this movement in *Eutaxia or the Presbyterian Liturgies* (1855), which included forms and prayers used in Strasburg, Geneva, and Edinburgh by the sixteenth-century reformers. These liturgies involved more congregational participation in worship and a better balance of prayer and praise and preaching. The Reverend John W. Nevin, a graduate of Princeton Theological Seminary and a colleague of Philip Schaff in Pennsylvania, was influenced by German Reformed theology and Romanticism. He wrote *The Mystical Presence* (1846) arguing for a return to Calvin's view of the "real spiritual presence" of Christ in the Lord's Supper. Others continued to retrieve and employ this rich Reformed heritage. Presbyterian musicians Thomas Hastings and Lowell Mason added to this movement.

Both the Old School and the New School produced some noted theologians. The New School professed its commitment to the *Westminster Standards* in the 1830s debate, and continued to hold to them, as did the Old School. Old School theologians such as Charles Hodge (1797–1878) of Princeton and James Henley Thornwell (1812–1862) of Columbia, South Carolina, continued to address problems of the Enlightenment in their writings. They did so with the help of what was called the Scottish "Common Sense" philosophy. This approach eschewed some speculative philosophic questions and sought to avoid such "isms" as materialism, idealism, skepticism, and other "isms." They emphasized freedom, self-evident moral intuitions, and genuine human agency and responsibility. In the process, they modified older concepts of Calvinism that were still debated among Presbyterians. At Union Theological Seminary in New York, Henry Boynton Smith, a convert from Unitarianism to New School Presbyterians, contributed to a Christocentric theology.

Presbygationalist Horace Bushnell (1802–1876) considered old problems with new insights about theological discourse, putting them in a fresh context. He explored different ways of knowing and of using language, making distinctions between the poetry of the Psalms and those parts of the Bible that were historical and doctrinal. He also stressed a "comprehensive" approach to theology in an attempt to bring persons of different perspectives to a higher level of discourse. While doing so, he emphasized Christ as the embodiment in life of God's forbearance and forgiveness and also as an example to believers through his vicarious sacrifice. In *Christian Nurture* (1847), his most popular book, Bushnell stressed the naturalness of childhood education in a Christian home and environment. Bushnell was attacked from various sides of doctrinal disputes, but he made a creative contribution to theological discussion through his exploration of methodological issues.

With regard to governance, however, Presbyterians of both schools also drew closer together. Members of the Old School, North and South, carried on important debates over some developments in Presbyterian polity. New School adherents still operated under the Plan of Union of 1801 and cooperated with Congregationalists. However, they began to define themselves more and more in terms of their Presbyterian connectional system and even began to develop their own denominational boards to carry out the problems of their General Assembly. Moreover, the Congregationalists, who under the Plan of Union often lost churches to the better organized Presbyterians, pulled out of the Plan of Union in 1852. They organized their own denomination, thus curtailing some of the cooperation of the two bodies.

At the same time, the Old School, North and South, continued the debate over governance. Hodge and Thornwell led the discussion about the role of the eldership. Hodge argued that elders, for all their importance, were only representatives of the people. They need not be ordained as were the clergy, and they were not essential to form a quota in church bodies to do the church's business. Thus Hodge took a position somewhat different than that of his colleague Samuel Miller. Thornwell opposed Hodge in these arguments. Although the church followed Hodge, the office of the eldership continued to grow in importance in the South and elsewhere. Old School adherents also discussed questions of the role of boards and other denominational agencies engaged to do the work of the church between meetings of the General Assembly. This problem came up in the church's attempt to deal with its mission obligations especially. Hodge argued, as did John Holt Rice of Union Theological Seminary in Virginia, that the whole church and every member in it constituted a mission society. The denomination, therefore, could organize boards to help it fulfill this and other responsibilities. They were not forbidden by the Bible. Thornwell argued that the boards were unscriptural and endangered the accountability of the Presbyterian representative system. The denomination followed Hodge again, and the General Assembly continued to organize its work under boards over which it maintained oversight. Hodge dubbed Thornwell's positions "hyper-*hyper*-HYPER-HIGH Presbyterianism." Thornwell returned the thrust, saying that Hodge represented "no, *no*, NO Presbyterianism." Thornwell's arguments provided a warning about the difficulty of supervising large organizations in an increasingly complex age. Old School agencies seemed to work more effectively than those of the New School at that time.

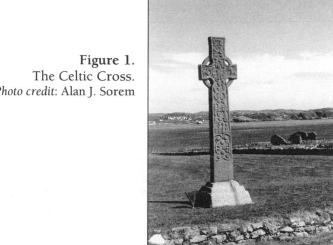

Figure 1.
The Celtic Cross.
Photo credit: Alan J. Sorem

Figure 2.
John Calvin as a
young man.
Photo credit: Parker,
John Calvin: A Biography.
Philadelphia:
The Westminster Press,
1975.

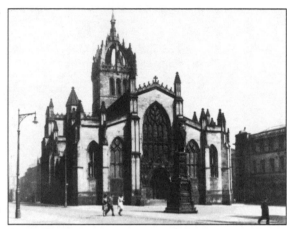

Figure 3.
St. Giles Cathedral,
Scotland.
Photo credit: Presbyterian Historical Society

Figure 4. John Knox.
Photo credit:
Presbyterian Historical Society

Figure 5.
Francis Makemie's trial in 1707
Photo credit:
Presbyterian Historical Society

Figure 6.
John Witherspoon.
Photo credit:
Presbyterian Historical Society

Figure 7.
Nassau Hall.
Photo credit: Princeton University Archives

Figure 8.
Revival (1800).
Photo credits: Old Dartmouth Historical Society,
Whaling Museum, New Bedford, Massachusetts,
and J. Maze Burbank

Figure 9.
Henry Highland Garnet.
Photo credit:
Presbyterian Historical Society

Figure 10.
Tent Meeting in California (1849).
Photo credit:
Presbyterian Historical Society

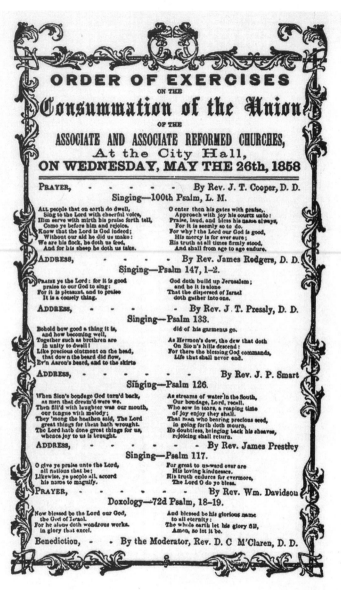

Figure 11.
Order of Exercises.
Photo credit: Presbyterian Historical Society

Figure 12.
Benjamin M. Palmer
(right) and the First
Presbyterian Church in
Augusta, Georgia
(below).
Photo credits:
The Historical Foundation,
Montreat, North Carolina
and Carl T. Julien

Figure 13.
Bethany Church, Philadelphia.
Photo credit: Presbyterian Historical Society

Figure 14.
First Women's Missionary Society in Idaho (1891).
Photo credit: Presbyterian Historical Society

Figure 15.
Louisa M. Woosley.
Photo credit:
Presbyterian Historical Society

Figure 16.
Grover ("the Good") Cleveland shows his political
creed to John ("the Pious") Wanamaker.
Photo credits: Judge, January 23, 1892.
The Collections of the Library of Congress

Figure 17.
Charles Parkhurst cutting off Tammany's tail.
Photo credits: *Puck*, November 7, 1894.
The Collections of the Virginia State Library

Figure 18.
The Witherspoon Building in Philadelphia
Photo credit: Presbyterian Historical Society

Figure 19. The Wilson Family (father and son).

Figure 20.
"The Lapsley."
Photo credit: The Historical Foundation,
Montreat, North Carolina

Figure 21.
John J. Eagan, businessman.
Photo credit: Courtesy of the
American Cast Iron Pipe Company

Figure 22. Francis Grimke.
Photo credit:

Figure 23.
(At right) Hallie P. Winsborough
and (below)
PCUS auxiliary (1912).
Photo credits:
The Historical Foundation,
Montreat, North Carolina

Figure 24.
First Women Elders (1931).
Photo credit: Presbyterian Historical Society

Figure 25.
Growing magazine (pastor and child) in 1948.
Photo credit: Presbyterian Historical Society

Figure 26.
Lois Stair, first woman
moderator (1971).
Photo credit:
Presbyterian Historical Society

Figure 27.
Eugene Carson Blake and Pope Paul VI (1969).
Photo credit: John Taylor, World Council of Churches,
Geneva, Switzerland

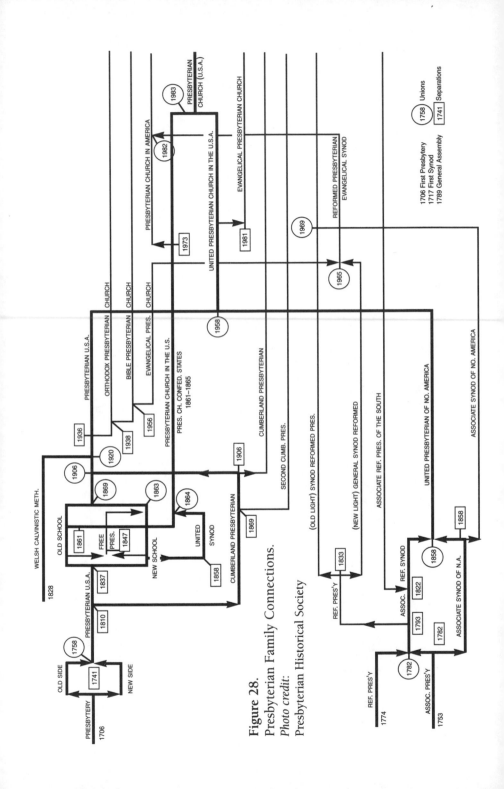

Figure 28.
Presbyterian Family Connections.
Photo credit:
Presbyterian Historical Society

Presbyterians built churches and missions across the continent. In 1836 physician Marcus Whitman and the Reverend Henry S. Spalding took to the Oregon Trail to set up mission stations and churches among the Cayuse Indians under the ABCFM. Their wives, Narcissa Whitman and Eliza Spalding, were the first white women to cross the continental divide. Whitman, accused by the Indians of causing a devastating epidemic of measles among them, was martyred, along with his wife and twelve other whites. The Spaldings continued to work among the new churches and Native Americans after the massacre.

The Cumberland Presbyterians were among the first in Texas. As already indicated, Sumner Bacon helped to establish there the first presbytery of that denomination. Sheldon Jackson began to plant churches in Wyoming, Montana, Idaho, Utah, and Arizona. He became known as the "Little Giant" of home missions. Thousands rushed to California after gold was discovered in the area. Missionaries Sylvester Woodbridge, Albert Williams, and James Wood—the three Ws—organized the first presbytery in the territory in 1850. The Reverend William Speer, who had already served as missionary to China, opened a mission in San Francisco in 1852 and established the first Chinese Presbyterian Church in the state in 1853. He offered pastoral assistance to the new immigrants and converts. Presbyterians of both schools also sent missionaries abroad under the ABCFM and the Board. The Honorable Walter Lowrie, former U.S. Senator of Pennsylvania, headed the Old School agency for a time, and the Reverend John C. Lowrie, a former missionary to India, succeeded his father in the post.

Civil War

Presbyterians could not repress debate over slavery, and, with it, the nature of the federal union. As did the U.S. Congress, they tried to gag those who wished to discuss the issue at meetings of church governing bodies. In 1787, and again in 1818, the General Assembly had condemned slavery and urged Presbyterians to work toward emancipation. Some constituents, for example, Charles C. Jones of Georgia and James Smylie of Mississippi, southern missionaries to slaves, began to defend slavery as a biblically sanctioned institution of labor. The Old School Assembly maintained that slave holding was no bar to communion. However, a New School missionary to Missouri wrote, in 1845, that slavery touched "every nerve and fibre of society," and acted like a "paralysis" to attempts to do good in America and the world.

Articulate African-American Presbyterians kept the issue before the public, as did Samuel Cornish and Theodore Wright. Henry Highland Garnet (1815–1882), an escaped slave, became a pastor, serving churches in Troy, North Carolina, New York City, and Washington, D.C. He was an outspoken critic of the system of slavery. He evoked biblical images of the United States as Egypt, a land of bondage, recalling rhetoric used by Presbyterians at the time of the revolution. He also saw America as a promised land, should its Declaration of Independence and Constitution be truly implemented. In indignation and defiance, he proclaimed to slaves at a public meeting in 1843, "Let your motto be resistance," thus causing anxiety among whites and even some blacks. Another African-American pastor, James W. C. Pennington of the First Colored Presbyterian Church in New York City, lectured widely, even in Europe, about his experience as a "fugitive blacksmith," and on the history of "Colored People," all in the name of liberty.

Even as whites attempted to avoid the issue, they became more and more divided. A layman, James Birney of Kentucky—a slave holder turned colonizationist turned abolitionist—held that the churches were *the* bulwark of slavery. He ran for president as head of the Liberty Party, which he helped to found. A few protesting Presbyterians left the church. Some Ohio Presbyterians, led by the Reverend John Rankin, abandoned the New School to form a Free Presbyterian Church. Another Buckeye State pastor, George Gordon, was jailed as a prisoner of conscience for joining an attack on a fugitive slave hunter. Presbygationalist Harriet Beecher Stowe gathered information and insight about slavery while her father, Lyman Beecher, and her husband, Calvin Stowe, presided over and taught at Lane Theological Seminary in Cincinnati. With her book *Uncle Tom's Cabin* (1851), she attacked slavery and became an instant celebrity. Her book inflamed the North, and infuriated the South. The novel was burned at Jefferson's University of Virginia. When President Abraham Lincoln welcomed her to the White House, he suggested that she was the little woman who brought on the sectional conflict.

The larger Presbyterian Church divided again, this time into four denominations. The New School split in 1858 when its General Assembly began a survey to see how its members were dealing with the issue of slavery. In 1858 New Schoolers in the South who favored slavery formed the United Synod of the Presbyterian Church in the United States of America. The Old School, however, managed to remain united until May 1861. When newly elected President Lincoln began to fortify Fort Sumter, South Carolina seceded from the Union and its militia fired on the federal installation. Soon other states followed suit and seceded. The General

Assembly, meeting in New York City, with a few southerners present, adopted the amended Gardiner Spring Resolutions. These resolutions called for prayer and fasting in the face of this national crisis and support for the federal government as defined by the Constitution, which Presbyterians helped write and under which they had lived for almost seventy-five years. But they did not identify the church with any particular administration or political party. A large number of commissioners, led by Charles Hodge protested. A gradual emancipationist with regard to slavery, Hodge charged that the General Assembly had unconstitutionally decided a political issue, the nature of national sovereignty. The General Assembly responded by calling this Civil War a case extraordinary. It admonished all to be subject to the federal government, brought in power in an election in which all Americans, including southerners, had just participated. It cited Paul's warning in Romans 13 about resisting legitimate civil authority.

Under these tragic circumstances, southern Presbyterians withdrew from the national assembly. They organized the General Assembly of the Presbyterian Church in the Confederate States of America, in Augusta, Georgia, in the winter of 1861. The new denomination adopted an "Address to the Christian World," written by Thornwell, which sadly observed that the General Assembly in New York had decided a political question contrary to the nature of the church, thus confusing "Christ and Caesar." It then admitted that slavery was the underlying root of the division and proceeded to defend slavery on biblical and philosophical grounds. Southerners then declared missions to be the great end of Christ's church, and elected the Reverend Benjamin M. Palmer (1818–1902) their first moderator.

The War between the States was a bloody fratricidal conflict. Old and New School Presbyterians, South as well as North, supported their own governments. They sent soldiers and chaplains into the fields of combat, and they helped organize the Christian Commission to minister to all those who bore the brunt of the long war. Both sides experienced revivals among combatants. The division of the churches produced sad consequences, however. The Reverend Leighton Wilson, a former missionary to Africa and a secretary of the Board of Foreign Missions in New York, returned home in the South. The Reverend Archibald A. Hodge, son of Charles Hodge, and a pastor in the Old Dominion, returned North with his Virginian wife Elizabeth. The Reverend William Anderson Scott, called from New Orleans to be pastor of the Calvary Presbyterian Church in San Francisco, misjudged his western congregation and friends. He began to pray publicly for two presidents, Jefferson Davis and Abraham

Lincoln. He offended the city's unionists and had to leave the city for his safety and that of his family.

Abraham Lincoln (1809–1865) had attended a Presbyterian Church in Springfield, Illinois, and rented a pew in the New York Avenue Presbyterian Church in Washington, D.C., where he worshiped. Apparently for theological reasons, he never joined the institutional church. Lincoln was steeped in Scripture and left a profound prophetic interpretation of the war in his Second Inaugural Address. After alluding to how the parties tried to avoid the war he came to the issue of slavery:

> One eighth of the whole population was colored slaves, not distributed generally over the Union, but localized in the southern part of it. These slaves constituted a peculiar and powerful interest. All knew that the interest was somehow the cause of the war. To strengthen, perpetuate, and extend this interest was the object for which this interest would rend the Union even by war, while the government claimed no right to do more than to restrict the territorial enlargement of it. Neither party expected for the war, the magnitude, or the duration, which it has already attained. Neither anticipated that the cause of the conflict might cease with, or even before, the conflict itself should cease. Each looked for an easier triumph, and a result less fundamental and astounding. Both read the same Bible, and pray to the same God; and each invokes His aid against the other. It may seem strange that any men should dare to ask a just God's assistance in wringing the bread from the sweat of other men's faces; but let us judge not that we be not judged. The prayers of both could not be answered; that of neither has been answered fully. The Almighty has His own purposes. "Woe unto the world because of offenses! For it must needs be that offenses come; but woe to that man by whom the offense cometh!" If we shall suppose that American Slavery is one of those offenses which, in the providence of God, must needs come, but which, having continued through His appointed time, He now wills to remove, and that He gives to both North and South, this terrible war, as the woe due to those by whom the offense came, shall we discern therein any departure from those divine attributes which the believers in a Living God always ascribe to Him? Fondly do we hope—fervently we do pray—that this mighty scourge of war may speedily pass away. Yet, if God wills that it continue, until all the wealth piled by the bond-man's two hundred and fifty years of unrequited toil shall be sunk, and until every drop of blood drawn with the lash, shall be paid with another drawn with the sword, as was said three thousand years ago, so still it must be said "the judgments of the Lord are true and righteous altogether."
>
> With malice toward none; with charity for all; with firmness in the right, as God gives us to see the right, let us strive on to finish

the work we are in; to bind up the nation's wounds; to care for him who shall have borne the battle, and for his widow, and his orphan—to do all which may achieve and cherish a just, and a lasting peace, among ourselves, and with all nations.

Reconstruction and Reunion

Philip Schaff wrote about the battle of Gettysburg near his home. He referred to the war as a "baptism of blood" for the nation. Horace Bushnell expressed similar sentiments. That river of blood left both sides bitter. The North became more bitter after Lincoln's assassination on Good Friday in 1865. Completing the work of the Emancipation Proclamation begun by Lincoln, the government freed slaves with the passage of the Thirteenth Amendment to the Constitution and then later extended rights of that freedom in the Fourteenth and Fifteenth Amendments to the Constitution. Henry Highland Garnet gave an oration in the House of Representatives, in Washington celebrating African-American liberation. Old School Presbyterians in the North insisted that southerners renounce, in repentance, the attempt of the South to secede, as well as the justification and practice of slavery. Northerners rubbed salt in the wounds by treating the South as a mission field, gathering African Americans into churches. They also started educational institutions for Blacks: Ashmun Institute in Oxford, Pennsylvania, and Biddle Institute in Charlotte, North Carolina. The UPCNA organized Knoxville College in Tennessee for freedmen.

In 1865 Southerners—defeated, desolate, yet defiant—organized the Presbyterian Church in the United States (PCUS) under a General Assembly, with a graduated system of governing bodies made up of clergy and ruling elders. It should be noted that the Old School and New School in the South had reunited in 1864. A northern loyalty oath aroused opposition among unionists in the border states of Kentucky, Missouri, and Maryland, where churches withdrew from the PCUSA, Old School, and related to the new denomination. The PCUS controlled two seminaries, Union Theological Seminary in Virginia and Columbia Theological Seminary in South Carolina, and a number of colleges, including an African-American school, now Stillman College. The General Assembly carried on its work through committees. It emphasized foreign missions, establishing churches in six different countries, including China. In 1866, the PCUS reported 65,588 members, 1,290 churches, and 829 ministers.

The Old School and New School in the north, which had cooperated during the war effort, finally reunited. Reunion in the north was aided by a growing ecumenical spirit among Calvinists and Christians in general. For example, Philadelphia businessman George H. Stuart organized a Pan-Presbyterian Convention in 1867 at his Reformed Presbyterian Church in Philadelphia. Members of the PCUSA, Old and New Schools, of the CPC, of the UPCNA, of the Dutch and German Reformed Churches, along with a few southerners from the PCUS, attended this meeting to further the cooperative spirit of the postwar years. In this spirit, the Old School and New School pressed ahead with plans to reunite under the leadership of Henry Boynton Smith of New York. They came together in Pittsburgh, in 1869, on the basis of the *Westminster Standards*, "pure and simple," indicating that some of the theological tension had dissipated during the years. *Harper's Weekly* called this reunion a great and solemn spectacle in ecclesiastical history. The reunited church reported 446,561 members, 4,526 churches, 4,238 ministers, and 448,857 Sunday school members.

Two other ecumenical bodies came into existence during those years. First meeting in Europe in the 1860s, the Evangelical Alliance was finally organized in America. This came about under the leadership of Philip Schaff, who had become a Presbyterian, and the Reverend Samuel I. Prime, another Presbyterian. The Alliance held a great international meeting in New York City in 1873, where Christians from the United States, the British Isles, and the continent met to discuss Christian cooperation, missions, and other challenges. Moreover, in 1876, those in the Reformed tradition organized another ecumenical body. This was the Alliance of the Reformed Churches throughout the World holding the Presbyterian System. This was accomplished with the help of Schaff and another Presbyterian, James McCosh, who was a Scot and the president of the Presbyterian College of New Jersey. Presbyterians of the South, however, reluctantly joined the Alliance. Moses Drury Hoge, of the Second Presbyterian Church of Richmond, argued vigorously on the floor of the General Assembly against those who resisted entrance into the Alliance. Southern Presbyterianism was not the last word from the Lord about Christ's church. Putting the matter in perspective he exclaimed: If "we alone constitute the true church; if this only is the result of the stupendous sacrifice on Calvary and the struggles of apostles, and missionaries and reformers in all generations; then may God have mercy on the world and on his church." His arguments persuaded his denomination to participate in the world body.

In 1876, Federal troops finally withdrew from the South, bringing "redemption" to the region. Political and ecclesiastical reconciliation continued afterward at a faster pace. Soon, southern Presbyterians were engaged in cautious "foreign correspondence" with other churches, and they gradually established formal fraternal relations with Presbyterians north of the Mason/Dixon line. While Americans continued to pick the scab of Civil War, healing had actually begun. Presbyterians could now turn their attention to a rapidly changing society with its industrialization, urbanization, and the intellectual challenges of the "Gilded Age."

9

The "Gilded Age" and an "Errand into the World"

As American extended its "errand into the world," Presbyterians faced challenges of new frontiers such as industrialization and urbanization, scientific and intellectual ferment, and international competition. The Reverend Professor Robert Ellis Thompson (1844–1924), socioeconomist of the University of Pennsylvania, published *A History of the Presbyterian Church in the United States* in 1895. He expressed the opinion that Presbyterians held "a place of great importance in the religious life of the nation" and had "weight beyond numerical strength." Presbyterian emphases on the life of the mind, theological discourse, personal and family discipline, and its "conservatism accounted for its influence on national life."

Despite what Thompson said about influence, Presbyterians were not of one mind about how to respond to these challenges. Different political allegiances point to a mixture of responses. Presbyterian President Grover Cleveland (1837–1908), a Democrat, served in office two terms, which was interrupted by the presidency of Presbyterian Benjamin Harrison (1833–1901), a Republican. While campaigning for office, Cleveland, the son of a minister, was accused of siring a child out of wedlock. He confronted the taunt: "Ma! Ma! Where's my Pa? Gone to the White House, Ha, Ha, Ha!" Although he was not sure of the paternity of the child, he did provide some support for the family. The Reverend Samuel Burchard, a Republican of New York City, did not make it easier for Cleveland among his Catholic supporters when the Presbyterian clergyman called the campaign a matter of "Rum, Romanism, and Rebellion." Later, Cleveland married Frances Folsom in the White House. Harrison, who taught Sunday school in a Presbyterian church in Indianapolis, while in office was accused of selling the government to the highest bidder. With his "Cross of Gold" speech—which was in support of silver—at the Democratic national convention in 1896, Presbyterian William Jennings Bryan (1860–1925), from Nebraska, extended his reputation as the great "Commoner." He also stirred opposition from his opponents.

In order to deal with the new demands of this period, Presbyterians developed new responses. They amended the *Westminster Confession,* expanded church agencies, such as those having to do with home and foreign missions, observed a denominational reunion, and supported several important ecumenical endeavors among Christians.

Industrialization, Urbanization, and the "Gilded Age"

Samuel L. Clemens (1835–1910), alias Mark Twain, fell under Presbyterian influences at home in Hannibal, Missouri. His mother had been converted by Ezra Stiles Ely, who traveled West to fulfill his ministry as a home missionary. With a collaborator, Twain published *The Gilded Age.* The title caught the spirit of the times with its expanding wealth and plutocratic influences in society and politics. Americans faced rapid industrialization, urbanization, and growth in riches, especially in the northeast and midwest. Many Americans migrated from rural to urban areas, whereas millions immigrated from all the nations of the world to become Americans. A Presbyterian industrialist of Philadelphia, Stephen Colwell, issued an early warning signal to the commonwealth with his book, *New Themes for Protestant Clergy* (1851). He wrote about the hardship people faced while adjusting to new demands on their lives, labor, and families in factories and city life. Colwell stated in the subtitle to his book that Christians were responding with "creeds without charity," "theology without humanity," and "Protestantism without Christianity." He endowed a new position of ethics at Princeton Theological Seminary so that students might be taught how to help parishioners face these problems. Toward the end of the century, the biblical interpreter Cyrus I. Scofield (1843–1921) from Mississippi took a different approach. A sometime Presbyterian-Congregational clergyman, he was a millennialist who believed that God's last dispensation was at hand. "God help us," he warned, "meet the seriousness of the days in which we live, with an apostate church, . . . a lost world, and an impending advent as our environment." In 1909, Oxford University Press published the popular *Scofield Reference Bible,* which laid out these pessimistic predictions of the future. Most Presbyterians in general rejected Scofield's prophetic message.

Presbyterian entrepreneurs, who have been called "industrial statesmen," also helped shape the age. The roll call includes persons such as

William E. Dodge, New York; Thomas Mellon, Pittsburgh; Cyrus Mc-Cormick, Chicago; Henry Gassaway Davis, West Virginia; Louis Severeance, Cleveland; Henry Flagler, Florida; Robert Dollar of California; and John J. Eagan, Atlanta and Birmingham. John Wanamaker, a premier retailer of Philadelphia, ran one of the largest Sunday schools in the country at Bethany Church. Andrew Carnegie, a Scottish immigrant who attended the Presbyterian church with his wife Louise, symbolizes the enormous creative energy of these men. While amassing a fortune, Carnegie published *The Gospel of Wealth* (1900), in which he defended individualism, private property, competition, accumulation, and plain hard work. By obeying such laws, he accounted for his riches. He also promoted philanthropy and he argued that the rich should not die rich, nor should they even bequeath huge sums to heirs who would then not need to work for a living. Wealth was to be used, according to Carnegie, as a trust from God. Some spouses of Presbyterian entrepreneurs who did inherit their husband's wealth became noted philanthropists. Margaret Olivia Sage (1828–1918) gave away approximately $80 million—a considerable amount—to Presbyterian causes, giving her a position as a benefactor comparable to the Rockefellers. Nettie Fowler McCormick (1835–1932) gave a considerable amount to the Chicago seminary named for her husband.

The "industrial statesmen" of the times have also been called "robber barons" because of "conspicuous consumption," and the shameful way they treated each other and those caught by the new economic system. The "Gilded Age" was shocked by the railroad strikes of 1877, the Haymarket Square bombing of 1886 in Chicago, and the Pullman riots of 1892–1893. These "earthquakes," with other labor unrest, exposed the repressive impact rapid development had on men, women, and children of the period. A Congregational journalist from England, William T. Stead, wrote a book about the windy city titled *If Christ Came to Chicago* (1894). He claimed that is Christ, the Man of Sorrows, were he to pay a visit, he would weep over the windy city as he had over the holy city of Jerusalem. Stead called for a "Union of all who Love in the Service of all who Suffer." Another Congregationalist, Charles Sheldon of Topeka, Kansas, wrote a novel that he titled *In His Steps* (1896). The chapters of this book were originally given as talks to young people. This book circulated widely. People began to ask Sheldon's question about the turmoil of the time: "What would Jesus do?" In another approach, Professor Robert Ellis Thompson offered an Augustinian vision in his book *De Civitate Dei—The Divine Order of Human Society* (1891), in which he championed the use of sociology to build a commonwealth without the economic materialism of socialism or capitalism. Charles Parkhurst, a contemporary of Thompson and pastor of the

Madison Square Presbyterian Church, New York, led a movement for better government and succeeded for a time in replacing Tammany Hall with a reform administration.

Many Presbyterians who helped shape the "Gilded Age" did support the economic emphases enunciated by Carnegie but not without some qualifications. Some attacked cut-throat competition, fraudulent practices, and the abuse of other human beings, including children. Charles Hodge of Princeton Theological Seminary wrote of the need to deal with the human misery, unrest, and violence caused by rapid accompanying industrialization and urbanization. Such an approach would also slow the spread of socialism and communism among Americans. Charles Stelzle, as he put it, rose up from the bowery in New York and became a Presbyterian clergyman. Knowing how the "other half" lived, he attempted to help Presbyterians bridge the gap between themselves and working families by starting a Working Men's Department (1903), later becoming the denomination's Department of Church and Labor. He also organized Labor Temple in New York City for ministry, especially with the immigrant population, and wrote a volume titled *The Gospel of Labor* (1912), in which he emphasized the dignity and purpose of work. In 1909, the denomination called the Reverend Warren H. Wilson to be Stelzle's assistant and to address the problems and needs of the rural church.

Presbyterians supported a number of social causes. They sought to protect Sunday as a day of rest for all, as well as prohibition of alcoholic beverages for the health of the whole society. Presbyterians also expanded their Sunday schools as already indicated. With regard to children, Patty Smith Hill, a Presbyterian in Louisville, Kentucky, pioneered kinder garten education in the 1880s and 1890s. She taught first in her native state, then as a faculty member of Columbia University's Teachers College. She taught America and the world to sing "Good Morning to All," better known in its later version as "Happy Birthday to You," which was set to music by her sister, Mildred J Hill. The song appeared in print in *Song Stories for the Kindergarten* (1893).

Presbyterians were concerned about reaching and teaching the "masses." In addition to expanding Sunday school missions and using "Uniform Lessons" with other denominations, Presbyterians developed urban evangelism, following a Chicago shoe salesman and revivalist, Dwight L. Moody (1837–1899). Moody set a pattern for urban revivals during those years. The Reverend Wilbur Chapman, for a time the pastor of John Wanamaker, became an itinerant preacher who popularized simultaneous revivals. He and other evangelists, such as Stelzle, addressed the needs of special groups in their audiences who congregated for spiritual uplift. John Converse, a manufacturer and banker of Philadelphia, helped establish an agency in the PCUSA for the promotion of evangelism by the denomination. Presbyterians also began the work of evangelizing and planting Sunday schools and churches among the immigrants, coming in great numbers from southern and eastern Europe, Italy, Hungary, Poland, and Asia.

Worship, Confessional Revisions, Intellectual Challenges

During this "Gilded Age," Presbyterians enriched their worship, modified their confessional standards, and wrestled with intellectual challenges. These challenges led to heresy trials among Presbyterians in the last decades of the century. Interest in liturgical renewal continued after the Civil War and culminated in the composition and adoption of *The Book of Common Worship* (1906) among Presbyterians. This development was due, in part, to requests of clergy for help in comforting congregations in time of personal crises. It also helped to satisfy tastes of more urbane congregations that were building more spacious buildings in Classical, Romanesque, and Gothic styles. Following liturgical trends in Scotland at the time, some of the PCUSA leaders, men such as Henry Van Dyke (1852–1933), a New York pastor, and Philadelphians, pastor Louis Benson (1855–1930) and layman Benjamin Comegys, formed a Church Service Society to address worship needs. This society proceeded to survey Presbyterians to determine concerns about worship. Although continuing to use the *Directory for Worship,* the denomination authorized the preparation of *The Book of Common Worship* (1906) for consideration. The book included orders and prayers for regular and special services, prayers for family worship, a "Treasury of Prayers," the Psalter, and a collection of ancient hymns and canticles for use in worship. Some people objected to this trend toward high churchism and the use of "canned prayers" as taking away the freedom of worshipers. Nevertheless, the volume was finally approved by the General Assembly "for voluntary use" in congregations. These words were also printed in bold type on the title page. The book was small enough for parishioners to carry with them for purposes of meditation. Other Presbyterian denominations did not move this far in liturgical development at that time, although they benefited from this effort. Louis Benson contributed to Presbyterian worship by editing *The Hymnal* (1895), a pioneering volume that embraced the whole history of Christian praise within its covers. Henry Van Dyke, who became a professor at Princeton University, composed the popular "Joyful, Joyful, We

Adore Thee, God of Glory, God of Love," which became a very popular hymn after it was set to the triumphant music of Beethoven's Ninth Symphony. Meanwhile, Thomas DeWitt Talmage (1832–1902) of the Central Presbyterian Church, Brooklyn, New York, packed people in with his flamboyant anecdotal preaching. His change in homiletic style was dubbed "Tal-magic." His presbytery, however, did not approve of his efforts.

At the same time, the PCUSA engaged in a debate about the *Westminster Confession,* which some Presbyterians wished to replace with a new confession or, at least, to amend. The CPC had already amended their standards dealing with the theological challenges of the times. These still had to do with the Calvinist statements about election, involving predestination and foreordination. In *Huckleberry Finn,* Mark Twain writes about a sermon Huck heard one Sunday on "preforeordestination." It was, according to Huck, the worst day of sermonizing he had ever experienced. One attempt of some in the PCUSA, in 1892, to revise the confession failed when three-quarters of the presbyteries would not grant what the majority of Presbyterians wanted. The debate continued even as Presbyterians celebrated the 250th anniversary of the Westminster Assembly. Later, a committee that included former President Benjamin Harrison and Associate Justice of the Supreme Court John Harlan, a member of the New York Avenue Presbyterian Church in Washington, D.C., recommended the addition of two chapters to the confession bearing the titles "Of the Holy Spirit" and "Of the Love of God and Missions." The new chapters covered two of the issues that Presbyterians had been debating and to which they had been trying to respond for several decades. Presbyterians addressed and classified their theological problems with statements about the work of the Holy Spirit in Christian experience, manifested in revivals, and God's love for the whole world as the basis of missions, which had grown so large during the great century of Christian expansion. These matters were also related to the old theological enigma of election. The denomination also dropped from the confession the sixteenth-century condemnation of "the Pope of Rome" as the "Antichrist."

At the same time, the church adopted a "Brief Statement of the Reformed Faith" in 1903. Henry Van Dyke, the principal author of these sixteen short articles, wrote in a more devotional and less speculative tone than the *Westminster Confession.* He subordinated sharper theological affirmations to the unifying purpose of love. These amendments and the "Brief Statement" were adopted, even though some opposed them as not adding anything to the confession, if properly interpreted. Presbyterians in the South were alarmed at these actions in the PCUSA. The PCUS passed a requirement that a change in the *Westminster Standards* required a three-fourths vote of the presbyteries for passage. Later in the 1940s, however, the denomination adopted a variation of these articles of faith.

Presbyterians produced a number of notable theologians and created several theological institutions. Charles Hodge published his massive, widely circulated, three-volume *Systematic Theology* (1871). By the time Hodge died in 1878, he had taught 3,000 students at Princeton Theological Seminary. At the same time, Robert Lewis Dabney (1820–1898) of Union Theological Seminary in Virginia published his *Systematic and Polemic Theology* (1871). A *System of Christian Theology*, by Henry Boynton Smith of Union Theological Seminary in New York, was published posthumously in 1884. William G. T. Shedd, of the same institution, published his two-volume *Dogmatic Theology* (1889). In the meantime, the PCUSA founded more theological institutions—Biddle Theological Seminary in Charlotte, North Carolina (1868), for African Americans; San Francisco Theological Seminary (1871), with the leadership of William Anderson Scott; and Lincoln Theological Seminary in Oxford, Pennsylvania (1871), also for African Americans. The PCUS developed similar institutions in Louisville, Kentucky (1893), in Austin, Texas (1902). It also founded what is now the Presbyterian School of Christian Education, for lay workers (1908), in connection with Union Theological Seminary in Richmond, Virginia. Those theological schools, as well as older seminaries, had to respond to intellectual challenges not always addressed in the massive tomes mentioned above.

Van Dyke alerted readers to spiritual challenges abroad in *The Gospel for an Age of Doubt* (1896). The first challenge had to do with the belief in the existence of God. Charles Darwin, with his research, reflection, and writing on the theory of evolution, seemed to threaten what has been called *doxological science*—science pursued for the glory of God. *Natural selection* seemed to undercut the argument about the ultimate purpose of creation, and thus a Creator, an argument that had been used for centuries to prove the existence of God. In his work, *What Is Darwinism?* (1874), Darwin denied God's mediational presence in an evolutionary universe. Charles Hodge objected to this reasoning and rejected aspects of Darwin's theory of evolution, charging him with atheism. Meanwhile, James McCosh (1811–1894), another Presbyterian, and president of the College of New Jersey, in Princeton, argued in *Development: What It Can and Cannot Do?* (1883) that evolution could be seen as God's handiwork. McCosh was joined in this view by other Reformed educators such as geologists Asa Gray of Harvard and James LeConte of the College of South Carolina, later of the University of California. These Calvinist geologists continued to practice doxological science, appropriating insights from the work of scientists such as Darwin. Presbyterian pastor and hymn writer, Maltbie D. Babcock, wrote a hymn in 1901 reassuring believers that "This Is My Father's World."

Presbyterians also had to face questions from scholars about the Bible. Higher Critics, as they were called, began to question the authorship of its books and raise questions about its accuracy. Is the Bible accurate, they asked, in psychological, physical or historical fact, and philosophical principle? In the face of this challenge to the Bible, the faculty at Princeton Theological Seminary defined and defended the truth, inspiration, and authority of Scripture as inerrant, or accurate, in these areas, as well as spiritual doctrine and moral duty. Some scholars, however, countered this approach. Professor Charles Briggs (1841–1913) of Union Theological Seminary in New York accused those who held the Princeton position with a kind of "bibliolatry." According to Briggs, the Princeton position was not that of the *Westminster Confession*. He argued that the critical method of studying and reading the Bible enhanced its divine message to the believer as the Holy Spirit testified in the heart to the truthfulness of God's witness in Jesus Christ through the Bible. Briggs, very conservative in his theology, was charged and tried for heresy and found guilty. He left the PCUSA. As a result of this controversy, Union Theological Seminary in New York also cut its official ties with the denomination. Meanwhile, Scofield said he would rather spend Sunday morning in a saloon than in a church listening to the preaching of a Higher Critic. Other scientists, in what became known as *the psychology of religion,* began to examine the psychological background of religious conversion, thus examining experiential claims about the work of the Holy Spirit witnessing to the Bible in the hearts and lives of believers.

Elizabeth Cady Stanton (1815–1902) printed *The Woman's Bible* (1895–1898) in which she and collaborators underscored how the Scriptures had been used to keep women in their places—subordinated to men. Stanton grew up in a Presbyterian household, but was drawn to Unitarianism because of its greater liberality toward women. Because she was bold enough to face the issue, she was viewed as a threat to the women's movement and many women dissociated themselves from this effort.

Governance, Missions, and a Reunion

Presbyterians had to adapt their representative system with regard to governance to the growing bureaucratic organizations in the "Gilded Age." The church reflected the trend in business enterprise and also in the growth of governmental services. Two PCUSA skyscrapers symbolized this development—156 Fifth Avenue, New York, became the office of the foreign mission enterprise, and the Witherspoon Building in Philadelphia housed such work as Christian Education, Home Missions, Pensions, and the offices of the General Assembly. Heretofore, the office of the Stated Clerk of General Assemblies had been clergymen who devoted themselves part time to the fulfillment of denominational duties. In the PCUSA, the Reverend William Henry Roberts (1844–1920) became the first Stated Clerk to fill the PCUSA position full time. Roberts became an expert on ecclesiastical law, editing *Laws Relating to Religious Corporations* (1908), still a valuable resource for all church leaders. In the PCUS, Joseph Ruggles Wilson, father of Woodrow Wilson, became Stated Clerk. He exercised considerable power and authority in General Assembly matters, although he continued to serve as a pastor. In addition, Presbyterians began to pay more attention to the financial support of clergy and their families. A PCUSA layman maintained, in 1869, that clergy deserved more than a scheme of charity on which to depend for bread. They had a "right," legally and logically, according to the writer, for a more generous support system and pensions especially for families and in old age. The Old School and New School had developed voluntary relief programs; however, neither program was very effective. The argument now shifted to one of equity and justice, not of parternalism and charity. In 1909, the PCUSA organized a sustenation fund, the first attempt of an American denomination to establish a contributory pension plan not dependent solely on benevolence. The CPC, the UPCNA, and the PCUS moved in similar directions during these years.

During this period, Presbyterian home and foreign missions grew as America possessed a continent, fighting the last Indian wars, buying Alaska in 1867, and annexing Hawaii in 1898. For example, PCUSA influence spread under the leaders of the Board of Domestic Missions. Cyrus Dickson was a persuasive orator and promoter, while Henry Kendall's vision covered the whole mission field as his parish. The audacious, energetic, and optimistic Sheldon Jackson (1834–1909) planted numerous churches along railroads in the prairie states and in the Southwest. In 1872, he launched his *Rocky Mountain Presbyterian* to report on his work in these areas. Traveling to Alaska to plant churches there, he also engaged in the education of Eskimos and attempted to preserve Alaskan culture, as the United States began to exploit the resources of the area. Sue McBeth (1830–1893) and her sister, Kate, carried on mission work among the Nez Perce Indians in Idaho. Although unordained, they conducted a school for the training of Native American ministers. Presbyterian missions to the Omaha Indians influenced the family of Joseph Le Flesche. His children became professional leaders in Native American enterprises: Frances became a noted anthropologist, and Susette, an author and Indian Rights activist, attempted to integrate her own religious Indian traditions with new Reformed faith and life. Susan LaFlesche Picotte (1865–1915), who became a physician, was the first American woman to be appointed as missionary by the PCUSA Board of Missions. Beginning in 1895, Donaldina Cameron waged a forty-two year struggle against the prostitution of Chinese girls in San Francisco. Jackson, the McBeth sisters, the LaFlesche family, and Cameron represent many others in Presbyterian denominations who labored in various home mission fields, planting Sunday schools as well as churches in rural areas, towns, and cities across the nation.

At the same time, foreign missions expanded the Presbyterian errand into the world under such leaders as Frank Ellinwood, Arthur Judson Brown, and Robert E. Speer (1867–1947) in the PCUSA, as well as others in the UPCNA, the CPC, and the PCUS. The reunion of the Old School and New School in 1869 brought some of the work of the ABCFM under the control of the new denomination. Reformed work expanded in the Middle East, represented by the growth of educational institutions including Roberts College in Constantinople and the American University in Beruit, Lebanon. The American University in Cairo was founded under the influences of the UPCNA. These institutions produced generations of leaders for the various countries in the area, as well as for the Christian family. In the Far East, missionaries to Korea, for example Lillias Stirling Horton, a physician, and her spouse Horace Grant Underwood, helped to organize "self-propagating," "self-supporting," and "self-governing" Christian churches, beginning the strong Presbyterian presence in that country. Along with other missionaries, they awakened a sense of national pride after the Japanese conquered and occupied Korea during those years. In the Congo, now Zaire, African-American William Sheppard and William Morrison served as missionaries of the PCUS. They discovered that the Kasai Company, a holding firm of King Leopold of Belgium, was abusing Africans on rubber plantations. In reporting these abuses to the public in the press, they stirred an international outcry against Belgium. Sheppard and Morrison believed the mistreatment of the Africans by a professedly Christian government kept Africans from hearing their message about Jesus. In 1909, a court trial exonerated both missionaries of the charge of slander. Mark Twain, not known for his affection for clergy, praised these missionaries. On the other side of the world, the Reverend Hampden C. DuBose campaigned vigorously against the opium traffic in China. By organizing the Anti-Opium League, he attracted much international attention. Finally, the Chinese government officially prohibited the opium traffic in that country. Thus Presbyterians spread the Gospel around the world in both word and work among people with whom they associated.

Women played an increasingly important role in both the church and missions through their many organizations. At this time, Presbyterians did not ordain women to the ministry of Word and Sacrament, although there was some agitation to do so. In 1889, a CPC presbytery did ordain Louisa L. Woosley (1862–1952), a talented and articulate woman, to the ministry. Her congregation needed her services and called her to preach because of her gifts. The General Assembly of her denomination, however, rejected this ordination but allowed Woosley to preach as an evangelist, which she did effectively for almost fifty years. She also wrote one of the first Presbyterian arguments for the ordination of women in *Shall Women Preach?* (1891).

Although they could not officially preach, Presbyterian women did make enormous contributions to Christian missions. As early as 1861, Sarah R. Doremus of the PCUSA began a process that led to the formation of the Women's Foreign Missionary Society (1870), guided by a Women's Executive Committee. Women entered the mission fields— home and foreign—as missionary spouses, single women, educators, doctors, and nurses. As true daughters of Dorcas, they performed duties on the fields that they were not allowed to do in their home congregations and presbyteries. Women published the accounts of their mission work in *Women's Work for Women* and *Home Missions Monthly,* and organized the World Day of Prayer, which became an occasion observed by Christians around the world. In the UPCNA, Sara Foster Hanna organized the General Missionary Society of that denomination in 1875. With the prodding of Eliza Clokey, this association started the Women's Annual Thank Offering, an event also joined by other Presbyterians and Christians in the work of missions.

Presbyterians began to grow more conscious of the needs of African Americans. George Washington Cable, a Presbyterian deacon and nationally known novelist of New Orleans, helped expose the infamous convict lease system and the impact of America's injustices to blacks in *The Silent South* (1885) and *The Negro Question* (1890). The Supreme Court of the United States of America added insult to injury, in 1896, when it handed down the decision known as *Plessy vs. Ferguson.* This case established a "separate but equal" approach to racial relations in the nation. Associate Justice John Harlan (1833–1911) was the lone dissenter. He declared the Constitution "color blind," and wrote that "there can be no doubt but that segregation has been enforced as a means of subordinating the Negro . . . and that the thin disguise of 'equal' accommodation . . . will not mislead anyone nor atone for the wrong this day done." Harlan's relative, Robert Harlan, was part African American.

Presbyterians attempted to work among African Americans after the Civil War, but they were separated in various ways: by denominations, synods, presbyteries, and congregations. In 1874, the CPC formed the Colored Cumberland Presbyterian Church (later the Second Cumberland Presbyterian Church). The PCUS was not too successful in its efforts, although it proclaimed that all God's children belong around the Lord's Table as members of one family. The denomination organized the Afro-American Presbyterian Church, in 1898, which later became the Snedecor Memorial Synod with four presbyteries. The PCUSA evangelized blacks more aggressively, especially in the South. An Afro-American Presbyterian Council was founded in 1894. Ministers, such as the Reverend Francis Grimke (1850–1937), of the Fifteenth Street Presbyterian Church, Washington, D.C., and Matthew Anderson, pastor of the Berean Presbyterian Church, Philadelphia, gave leadership to the Council. The *African American Presbyterian* periodical expressed black Presbyterian concerns. Lucy Craft Laney (1854–1933), a black educator, founded a school for African-American children in Augusta, Georgia, and championed such education in the work of the denomination. The PCUSA segregated African Americans in the synods of Catawaba, Atlantic, Canadian, and Blue Ridge until the 1950s, when the PCUS and the PCUSA did away with their racial and ethnic synods. In the intervening years, African-American Presbyterians fought against this segregation in Christ's body.

The PCUSA welcomed some Germans with a few Swiss and Dutch immigrants who moved into the upper Midwest and organized a congregation in Iowa in 1854. This and other German-speaking congregations started Dubuque Theological Seminary, whose graduates preached in German and published German-language publications. In 1912, these congregations formed the all-German Synod of the West, which continued until it was assimilated in the 1950s.

Reunion, a Parliament of Religions, and a Council of Churches

Presbyterians continued the work of healing their own divisions and engaged in other ecumenical projects. The PCUSA and the CPC cooperated through the work of the Evangelical Alliance and the Alliance of Reformed

Churches during those years. Some members of the CPC held that the confessional revisions of 1903 in the PCUSA satisfied the difficulties that they had with the *Westminster Confession,* whereas some members of the PCUSA felt that the CPC had so modified their approach to theology that a reunion was not desirable. Nevertheless, these bodies, separated for almost one hundred years, reunited in 1906. The provisions of the reunion allowed for segregated congregations, black or white, wherever people wanted to organize them. The Reverend Francis Grimke was joined by Justice Harlan in casting votes against the reunion in the Washington, D.C., presbytery because of this provision of the plan. Almost one-third of Cumberland Presbyterian congregations remained outside of this ecumenical endeavor. Since the CPC had strength in border states and in the South, the PCUSA became more of a national denomination. In 1907, the new body listed 1,165,915 adherents, 9,031 pastors, and 1,657,747 involved in Sunday school.

Presbyterians during this period were engaged in the organization of a number of ecumenical meetings and organizations. They made considerable contributions in a spirit of Christian cooperation. In connection with the Chicago World's Fair that was officially opened by Grover Cleveland in 1893, Presbyterian John Henry Barrows (1847–1902) helped plan the World Parliament of Religions. Barrow's committee invited representatives of major world religions to gather in Chicago to represent the unity of the human family and to share religious views with one another and with the world. Notable religious leaders accepted this invitation. The General Assembly of the PCUSA condemned the gathering, thinking that the Parliament compromised Christian faith. However, several notable Presbyterians from around the country participated, believing that this gathering was important for Christian mission, for American society, and for human relations in general. Barrows thought of his involvement as a form of evangelism, and he invited Buddhists to his congregational worship where he preached about "Christ the Wonderful!" In his address at the Parliament, the aging and ailing Philip Schaff called for the "Reunion of Christendom,"—Orthodox, Catholic, and Protestant. He believed such reunion would help Christians in their mission to the world. He called for the pope to convene an ecumenical council in Jerusalem to deal with this yearning for reunion and more faithful witness.

Frank Ellinwood, of the PCUSA mission board, and other Presbyterians had begun to take the study of comparative religion seriously for mission purposes, and the Parliament was an impetus in this direction. Ellinwood was a founder of the national Society for the Study of Comparative Religion. Later, a great missionary conference was held in

New York City in 1900, presided over by honorary chair, Benjamin Harrison. This was attended by missionaries of all denominations from all over the world, to share with one another reports on the results of their work. The conference attracted a large number of people and manifested the growth of a worldwide Christian community.

In 1908 American Protestantism took a step toward greater cooperation by organizing the Federal Council of Churches of Christ (FCC) in America. Some had grown dissatisfied with the Evangelical Alliance, a voluntary society of individual Christians who were interested in Christian cooperation and unity. Supporters of the FCC believed denominations had a corporate responsibility to cooperate in meeting the challenges of the age. Thirty American denominations, with a membership of more than seventeen million formed his body. While adhering to their own confessional traditions, these denominations promoted, among other things, the *applied Christianity* movement, or the *Social Gospel*, as it was also called by those concerned about the special problems inherited from the nineteenth century. They believed that those who served together would grow together. The purpose of the organization was to manifest the oneness of the body of "Jesus Christ," confessed as "divine Lord and Savior," and to promote fellowship, evangelism, and a witness to the Kingdom of God—all those things that could be done better through cooperation than by separated denominations. It did not involve discussion of denominational union. Presbyterian minister Samuel J. Niccolls of St. Louis, Missouri, made the body decidedly evangelical by introducing the word "divine" before "Lord and Savior" in the brief confessional statement of the council, thus excluding nontrinitarians. William Henry Roberts chaired the FCC in 1908 when the ecumenical body convened.

The PCUSA, the UPCNA, and the PCUS, sent delegates to the first meeting of the FCC. The interdenominational council benefited Presbyterians because it brought them into contact with other denominations including bodies that were more racially, socially, economically, and politically diverse. The new council adopted what was called the *Social Creed* of the churches, which called on Christians to deal with the challenges of America's industrial and urbanized society. The PCUSA adapted and adopted a version of this statement in 1910. It stressed how important it was for Christians to consider wealth as a trust and to work for an equitable distribution of riches. It also called for fair wages and fair working hours, for safe working conditions, for some kind of social security for old age, and for the abatement of poverty. In sum, the creed endorsed the effort to make America a more just and compassionate nation.

The PCUS membership in the FCC was intermittent; however, some members carried out the vision of the council in their lives and ministries. For example, Elder John J. Eagan, of American Cast Iron Pipe Company, tried to implement some of the FCC's recommendations in his business, while the Reverend Alexander McKelway led a movement for national legislation curbing the use of children in the labor force. Woodrow Wilson (1856–1924), an elder in the PCUS, ran for the presidency on a platform of reform. In his book *The New Freedom* (1913), he declared:

> We stand in the presence of a revolution—not a bloody revolution; America is not given to the spilling of blood—but a silent revolution, whereby America will insist upon recovering in practice those ideals which she has always professed, upon securing a government devoted to the general interests and not to special interests.

Wilson, as president, supported Eagan's and McKelway's efforts to promote peaceful reform. Together they represented a "higher realism," which manifested compassion in the quest for justice, to use the term of Presbyterian elder and Wilson scholar, Arthur Link. So, some Presbyterians faced the challenges in the nation and in the world during the "Gilded Age" and at the dawn of the twentieth century.

10

From World War I
to World War II

In the amendment to the *Westminster Confession* in 1902, "Of the Gospel of the Love of God and Missions," the PCUSA expressed a world-wide vision of the Christian faith and life:

> God in infinite and perfect love, having provided in the covenant of grace, through the mediation and sacrifice of the Lord Jesus Christ, a way of life and salvation, sufficient for and adapted to the whole last race of man, doth freely offer this salvation to all men [and women] in the gospel. In the gospel God declares his love for the world and his desire that all men should be saved.

The Presbyterian confession about the world was adopted as the United States emerged as a world power. The world was anything but a place of love during the years from the Spanish-American War through World War I and World War II. The nation fought the Spanish-American War in Cuba, Puerto Rico, and the Philippines, then extending U.S. territory. The PCUSA General Assembly accepted this war as an opening for new fields for Christian endeavors for Protestants, although some Presbyterians opposed the American expansionism. William Jennings Bryan and Henry Van Dyke attacked this imperial adventure as a danger to American civilization, which they thought should be dedicated to the enlightenment, not the subjugation of the world.

In the second decade of the new century, Americans fought World War I, faced the illusions of the "Roaring Twenties," the disillusions of the world Depression, and then fought World War II. From this last struggle, the United States emerged victorious as a global superpower. Presbyterians participated in these events, which in turn helped shape their Christian faith and life as they sorted their theological convictions, reorganized denominational structures, and ministered to the nation's and the world's wounds.

World War I

A decade after the founding of the Federal Council of Churches (FCC) and early attempts of Presbyterians to meet some of the problems of the industrial revolution, Americans became embroiled in World War I in Europe. Woodrow Wilson, son of Joseph Ruggles Wilson, served as president of Princeton University and as governor of New Jersey. As a Democrat, he ran for and was elected to the office of President of the United States. He devoted his attention, after 1912, to the economic problems of the nation by stressing "New Freedoms" of economic responsibility, as already indicated. When war broke out in Europe, Wilson attempted to keep the nation out of the conflict. He failed in this endeavor, however, finally asking Congress to declare war on Germany in 1917 "to make the world safe for democracy," drawing on ideas deep in the American grain. He rallied the country by proposing war aims in "Fourteen Points." These included the right of self-determination of peoples and a world organized after the war under the covenant of a League of Nations. He believed the League would help the world deal with all the problems which would remain in the wake of the war. Although a great president in many ways, he was unable to lead the nation into the League after all grew "quiet on the western front."

Officially and unofficially, Presbyterians supported the war effort as "just and necessary," and some even helped to turn the conflict into a crusade. The conflict, which introduced trench and sea warfare and weapons such as machine guns and tanks and submarines, caused horrendous death and destruction in parts of Europe. Flamboyant William "Billy Sunday" (1863–1935), former baseball player turned Presbyterian revivalist, recruited for the armed services and sold war bonds on the "sawdust trail." "If you turn hell upside down," he proclaimed, "you will find 'Made in Germany' stamped on the bottom." On another occasion, he declared, "I tell you it is Bill [Kaiser Wilhem] against Woodrow, Germany against America, Hell against Heaven." Robert E. Speer, of the Presbyterian Foreign Mission Board, saw the conflict in more sober terms. He served as chair of the wartime commission of the FCC, which coordinated Protestant efforts during the war—for example, in the support of chaplains who served in the armed forces of the country. In one address, he warned Americans against self-righteousness and cautioned against the dangers of turning America into a "nationalistic sect." He urged moderation of spirit in the conduct of a war that he thought was just and necessary, but that was also a commentary on the sinful human condition. Because of his cautionary remarks, some critics questioned his patriotism. Presbyterians officially supported Wilson's war aims, especially the League of Nations.

Instead of making the world safe for democracy, the war turned nations to Facism and Naziism, and to Communism during the Russian Revolution of 1917. Some Presbyterians, appalled by the devastation of the war, turned to pacifism. In the PCUSA an attempt was made to remove from the *Westminster Confession* the provision allowing Christians to go to war on "just and necessary occasions." This move, however, failed in the churches in 1939, just as World War II exploded in Europe.

"Roaring Twenties"
and Depression

Meanwhile, Presbyterians had to confront the "Roaring Twenties" and the stock market crash of 1929, after which the country and the world plunged into a prolonged Depression in the 1930s. During the last years of Wilson's administration, Americans ushered in the 1920s by adding two amendments to the Constitution. The Eighteenth Amendment (1919) inaugurated the era of the "Prohibition of the manufacture, sale, or transportation of intoxicating liquors" in the United States of America. The temperance movement, well over a hundred years old, had reached its climax. Many Presbyterians and General Assemblies supported movement, as well as the amendment. The experiment was well intentioned and did decrease the consumption of alcohol. However, it represented a misguided approach to social control. Americans, including Presbyterians held different attitudes toward the use of alcoholic beverages. The experiment was repealed in the 1930s.

In the Nineteenth Amendment (1920), Americans finally recognized women's right to vote. The amendment was the climax of another long movement, which extended back at least to the 1840s. Not all Presbyterian men and women, however, supported this amendment. The Reverend Professor James Woodrow, uncle of Wilson, who had been disciplined by the PCUS for supporting a modified view of evolution, opposed this expansion of women's involvement in public affairs. Should women be allowed to vote, he warned in the late 1870s, "there will be no longer a South worth living for or worth dying for." As President, nephew Wilson supported the amendment, somewhat reluctantly at first, and then celebrated its enactment with the champions of the women's movement.

A number of prominent laity also shaped the 1920s. Congregational layman Bruce Barton, wrote an extremely popular book, *The Man Nobody Knows* (1925). He depicted Jesus as the most successful entrepreneur, a genius, who took twelve disciples and molded them into the greatest business enterprise in the world. Billy Sunday, the man's man, the ex-baseball player, continued to preach revivals with his robust masculine Gospel to

112 A BRIEF HISTORY OF THE PRESBYTERIANS

save America's soul from the age of the "Flapper." Some business executives figured out that Sunday saved more souls at a cheaper rate than did any of the churches in America. William Jennings Bryan, almost elected president of the United States and almost elected moderator of the PCUSA, traveled to Tennessee in 1925. He fought and won the Scopes Trial. A law which forbade the teaching of evolution in the public schools of the state. He won the battle but not the war. For his troubles, H. L. Mencken dubbed him the "Fundamentalist Pope." Although Mencken probably included Bryan in his species of "Boobus Americanus," neither he nor others did justice to Bryan's influence as the great "Commoner" and democratic leader. Meanwhile, a Presbyterian, Andrew Mellon, as secretary of the treasury, along with other Presbyterians, helped direct America's economic life. Scottish Presbyterian immigrant and businessman, B. C. Forbes, dispensed financial and moral advice in such publications as *Forbes Epigrams* (1922) and *Keys to Success* (1926). "Pray, yes," he suggested, "but when you get off your knees, don't sit down. Hustle!" With the help of the laity, Presbyterians organized a New Era Movement (1919–1923) for church promotion, and also joined with other denominations in the support of the Interchurch World Movement to promote Christianity around the globe. This latter program fell short of its financial goals.

Presbyterians also moved to reorganize boards and agencies that had proliferated through the years. They tried to make the church more efficient and effective. Church leaders who had been largely preacher-teachers were now taking on the responsibilities of church administration at various levels of the denomination's life. Between the years 1920 and 1923, the General Assembly of the PCUSA approved consolidation of all its work, including that of the women, into four Boards: Foreign and Home Missions, Education, and Relief and Sustentation. The UPCNA went through a similar process, which was not completed until 1928. Southern Presbyterians also reorganized their committees, but they did not consolidate their work until the 1940s, when they organized the Boards: World Mission, Church Extension, Education, Annuities, and Women's Work.

This process of consolidation produced unintended consequences in the PCUSA, especially with regard to the service and status of women in the church. By 1915 the PCUSA allowed women to be elected as deaconesses. In the reorganization, however, well-intentioned males prevailed and presided. They subordinated the large and successful women's mission work and boards to male control. Thus they deprived women of the leadership posts through which the women had built highly successful mission work. Katherine Jones Bennett (1864–1950) and Margaret

Hodge, representatives of women in the reorganization process, complained about this arrangement. They objected to the fact that women could not serve as clergy or elders and thus participate in the control and direction of this work. Bennett and Hodge surveyed and published their findings, in 1927, in a report titled "Causes of Unrest among the Women of the Church." Because of the unrest, the denomination did vote to ordain women as ruling elders, thus involving them in the governance of the denomination and the agencies to which women had made such a large contribution through the years. The first women ruling elders were elected and served in the General Assembly of 1930. The PCUSA did not approve of the ordination of women to the ministry of Word and Sacrament at this time. In 1926, Hallie Winsborough (1865–1940) of Kansas City, head of the Women's Auxiliary of the PCUS, was finally allowed to give her report about the work of her agency in person to the southern General Assembly.

Presbyterians also faced serious theological tensions in the debate between liberals and conservatives during this period. In the nineteenth century, Presbyterians wrestled primarily to restate some of the tenets of Calvinism. The intellectual challenges of the early part of the twentieth century involved more central issues having to do with the authority of the Scriptures and the person and work of Jesus Christ over life and the world. The controversy tended toward a reductionism and polarization of the issues and debate. Liberals, sometimes called Modernists, accepted the critical study of the Bible, as well as many of its findings. They emphasized God's immanence, Jesus as the manifestation of God's love and forgiveness, and Jesus as a prophet of God's Kingdom of Justice, toward which humans, by God's grace, could make progress. Professor William Adams Brown (1865–1943) of Union Theological Seminary, New York, did this from a liberal point of view in *Christian Theology in Outline* (1906). In response, "Fundamentalists," as they were called, set forth brief statements at General Assemblies of the PCUSA in 1910, 1916, and 1923, as "essential and necessary" articles to protect the faith. They included the inerrancy of the Bible, the virgin birth of Christ, the substitionary atonement (that Christ died for our sins), the physical resurrection of Christ, and Christ's imminent physical Second Coming. These articles were seen as binding on all ordained leaders of the church and were popularized in *The Fundamentals: A Testimony to the Truth* (1909), which was published by two California laymen, Lyman and Milton Stewart. They distributed an estimated 2,500,000 copies free of charge. The articles had not been submitted to the presbyteries for approval by the General Assembly, however. Consequently, some leaders of the church threatened to leave the church over what appeared to them to be unconstitutional acts of the General Assembly. They declared their faithfulness in theology in "An Affirmation" (1924), popularly known as the "Auburn Affirmation."

Irenic, conservative Charles Erdman of Princeton Theological Seminary was elected the moderator of the church in 1925. He appointed a commission to study this unrest in the church. The commission reviewed Presbyterian history. In 1927, it presented a report that reminded members of the Adopting Act of 1729 and of other agreements made throughout the history of the denomination. Although it did not emphasize polity over theology, it did reaffirm that the General Assembly could not define the "essential and necessary" articles of faith in the way that it had done previously. The General Assembly reaffirmed the freedom that allowed presbyteries to determine what was or was not outside the bounds of orthodoxy established by the denomination. This process had been part of the Presbyterian system since the eighteenth century. It should be noted that neither Liberals nor Fundamentalists in the Presbyterian Church were as reductionist as they sometimes sounded and were more generous in their sentiments than they sometimes acted. The controversy persisted, however. UPCNA leaders, concerned that the *Westminster Confession* was falling into disuse, prepared a brief statement, following the 1903 effort of the PCUSA. This statement was written in contemporary modern language, liberalizing emphases made in the seventeenth-century document. The United Presbyterians made another statement in 1925, declaring that the *Westminster Standards* of the 1640s should not be the last word uttered by Presbyterians about God and human nature and destiny.

This debate spilled over into the work of the denominations in foreign missions. Laity had been strongly engaged in the support missions through the decades. In the 1930s some of them engaged in a worldwide investigation of the impact of the work of the church in this field and began the task of "rethinking missions." The results were published as the *Laymen's Foreign Missions Inquiry* (1932), which stressed the need for Christians to witness to Christ by demonstrating Christian love through mission institutions such as schools, hospitals, and other agencies of Christian philanthropy. The missionaries were advised to spend more time understanding the non-Christian religions of the world. Presbyterians accepted some of the criticisms of the *Laymen's* report while rejecting others. Pearl Buck, noted author and Nobel prize winner for *The Good Earth* (1931), was a missionary with the Presbyterian mission to China, a country about which she wrote with such affection and effect. Due to the pressure of this controversy, she left the PCUSA board because of her sympathy with the *Laymens'* inquiry. Sam and Jane Higginbottom, agricultural missionaries to India, were attacked for abandoning evangelism for the "Gospel of the Plow." They had "Higginbottomized" the Gospel. The couple witnessed by teaching hungry Asians how to farm and feed themselves. The PCUSA General Assembly elected Sam moderator in 1939, during a furlough, affirming his approach as one way to spread the Gospel. Robert E. Speer broadened Presbyterian sympathies and witness about race relations in America and world missions through his work *Of One Blood* (1924). He also produced another volume titled *The Finality of Christ* (1933) in which he explored other faiths. However, he affirmed the uniqueness of Jesus Christ and God's love for the world. Some conservatives, such as Professor J. Gresham Machen (1881–1937), a colleague of Erdman at Princeton Theological Seminary, along with other conservatives, left that institution because of this conflict. He was disciplined by the PCUSA for starting an independent Board of Missions. He founded Westminster Theological Seminary and the Orthodox Presbyterian Church (OPC) in 1936. Because of disagreements in that body, the Reverend Carl McIntire left the OPC and proceeded to found the Bible Presbyterian Church in 1938.

Although the Presbyterian church experienced division in this period, some Presbyterians were broadening the interreligious dialogue to include Jews and Roman Catholics in America. The National Conference of Christians and Jews was founded in 1927 to deal with religious tensions. The Reverend Everett R. Clinchy, a Presbyterian minister, served as executive of the conference for years. The Reverend Samuel Macrae Cavert (1888–1976), a Presbyterian minister and executive of the FCC, contributed to the work of this body. After visits to Europe prior to World War II, Cavert alerted American Christians of the dangers of Naziism, Fascism, and growing anti-Semitism. The PCUSA condemned this anti-Semitism in its denominational statements.

The Depression, beginning in 1929, jolted the world economic system, as well as the lives of many Americans. It also stimulated Presbyterians to pursue economic justice in the society during the 1930s. The PCUSA called on the country to do away with unemployment, supply self-respecting jobs for all Americans, provide sanitary and livable dwellings, provide some kind of social insurance, and to protect Americans against social illness, injuries, and the infirmities of old age. In 1934, the General Assembly called for "new motives," besides those of "money-making and self-interest," which would change the social order, repeating concerns expressed in the first decades of the century. In 1936, as hardship persisted, the denomination set up a Department of Social Education and Action to address human misery by implementing these suggestions. Norman Mattoon Thomas (1884–1968), grandson of Presbyterian missionaries to Thailand, son of a Presbyterian minister, and a Presbyterian minister himself for a time, was a standard bearer of the Socialist Party during these years.

The PCUS tended to avoid social, economic, and political issues because these were not related to the Christian spirituality that the denomination emphasized. However, southerners also felt the bite and bitterness of Depression. Presbyterians believed that they had a responsibility to deal with what was wrong with the economic and political order. So in 1936, under progressive leaders including Professor Ernest Trice Thompson (1894–1995) of Union Theological Seminary in Virginia, the denomination established a Committee on Moral and Social Welfare. For the first time, the denomination adopted a *Social Creed,* similar to that of the FCC, adapted to the needs of the South and the nation. Many Presbyterian ministers, though generally moderately conservative, supported some of the provisions of the New Deal including Social Security legislation to deal with the growing insecurity experienced by many Americans. Actor James Stewart, a Presbyterian, was a hit in "Mr. Smith Goes to Washington" (1939) in which he faced the harsh realities of American politics.

Presbyterian spirits were lifted during this period of stress—and later—by the work of Clarence Dickinson (1873–1969), organist and musical director of Buck Presbyterian Church, and his spouse Helena Dickinson (1875–1957). In 1928 the Dickinsons organized the School of Sacred Music at Union Theological Seminary, New York. In the 1920s, John Finley Williamson directed the Westminster Choir at the Westminster Presbyterian Church in Dayton, Ohio, and built the Westminster Choir College, Princeton, New Jersey, in 1932. These musicians and institutions enhanced appreciation for sacred choral tradition for Christians of all denominations. Presbyterians William and Ann Lee Willet of Pittsburgh, founded the Willet Stained Glass Studio to lift the human spirit with the art of stained glass. Their son Henry Lee Willet, and his spouse Muriel, carried on this ministry in Germantown, Pennsylvania. Later, Henry contributed his insights to the work of the church by serving as a member of the Board of Christian Education in Philadelphia.

World War II: "V" for Victory and Violence

World War II broke out in 1939. European nations finally declared war on Germany for Nazi aggression. After Japan's attack on Pearl Harbor in 1941, the United States entered the global conflict. Presbyterians, along with other Christians, considered the war just and necessary, and thus supported the war effort. They did so, however, without the crusading zeal that had marked participation in World War I. Now they tried harder to be guided by purposes justified on Christian grounds. Presbyterians joined other Christians in the FCC in developing war aims. John Foster Dulles (1888–1959), a Presbyterian minister's son and noted Wall Street lawyer, headed a Commission to Study the Basis of a Just and Durable Peace. The commission issued "Guiding Principles" and "Six Pillars of Peace." These statements called Christians to affirm faith in God and a moral international order, to reject hypocrisy, hate, and the desire for revenge in approaching lasting peace, and to promote a United Nations to help the world after the war to deal with future political, economic, and religious conflicts. Presbyterians in the PCUSA, PCUS, UPCNA, and the CPC each supported these war aims, including the formation of the United Nations—the unfulfilled dream of Woodrow Wilson.

Presbyterians were shocked, as were all other denominations, by the dropping of the first atomic bombs on Japan. The use of bombs helped bring the war, with all its human and physical waste and the erosion of moral norms, to an end. But some believed that while the development of the bombs illustrated the ingenuity of the human mind, dropping the bombs, however, demonstrated the inhumanity of human beings to one another. Henry Stimson, secretary of war and a Presbyterian, explained after the war that the use of the bombs was simply the last of a long list of horrendous decisions he and other policymakers had had to make and carry out during the conflict. Arthur Holley Compton, of a noted Wooster College, Ohio family, a winner of a Nobel Prize for physics, and a Presbyterian elder, had helped to direct the Manhattan Project in Chicago that ushered in the Nuclear Age. After the war, Compton was called to Washington University in St. Louis as chancellor. He devoted the rest of his life to education for the atomic era. Meanwhile, the wisdom of the use of the bombs continued to be debated.

Dulles, who helped guide Protestant and Presbyterian discussions of a "just and durable peace" during the war, was a leading participant in the organization of the United Nations in 1945 and represented Presbyterian support of the organization. In 1947 Presbyterian churches supported the Universal Declaration of Human Rights adopted by that body. After the war, Presbyterians developed programs and collected special funds to help rebuild Christian institutions throughout the world and the nation. In the PCUSA, the Restoration fund collected and distributed over $25 million for rebuilding in Europe and Asia after the war. John Leighton

Stuart, a missionary to China, served as ambassador to China, a wartime ally, in the 1940s. He guided American policy until the postwar revolution in that country.

Presbyterians were assisted in dealing with these events of the 1930s and 1940s by a fresh theological movement often referred to as *Neo-Orthodoxy*. This movement actually began in the discouragement and despair of World War I, the Depression, and during the German church's struggle with Naziism. This produced the famous *Theological Declaration of Barmen*, affirming that "Jesus Christ is Lord," in a challenge to the modern totalitarian state. Theologians Karl Barth and Emil Brumner were among the most notable European leaders of the movement. American theologians, Reinhold Niebuhr (1892–1971) of Union Theological Seminary in New York, and H. Richard Niebuhr (1894–1963) of Yale Divinity School, clergy of the Evangelical and Reformed Church, contributed to this theological renaissance. As Nazi bombs began to fall on Britain in 1939, Reinhold gave lectures later published as *The Nature and Destiny of Man* (1941). Later, in *The Children of Light and The Children of Darkness* (1944), he vindicated the need for democracy, restating the arguments of Witherspoon and Madison: "Man's capacity for justice makes democracy possible; man's inclination to injustice makes democracy necessary." H. Richard wrote on the Christian story in *The Meaning of Revelation* (1941) and *Christ and Culture* (1951), about nature and grace, and the call to Christians in the light of grace to engage in the transformation of culture. They brought both Lutheran and Calvinist traditions, represented by their denomination, into the theological conversation. This movement helped some people deal with the legacy of the Liberal-Fundamentalist controversy.

Neo-Orthodoxy was first of all a biblical theology. While this view accepted many of the conclusions of modern biblical scholarship and acknowledged the relativity of culture and human aspirations, the Bible was held as the self-revelation of God to human beings, the Word of God spoken especially in the life, death, and resurrection of Jesus Christ. With fresh vitality, Neo-Orthodoxy, or Neo-Reformation, reemphasized the great doctrinal affirmations of the Christian people, especially God's transcendence, human finitude and sinfulness, and the need for redemption by the grace of God. This need was highlighted for many by World War II, the Holocaust of the Jews, and the dropping of the first atomic bombs. These earth-shaking events raised serious questions about the idea of progress as well as optimism about the human condition. Theologians who articulated these theological ideas realized the paradoxical nature of human existence and its existential character. Humans receive the action of God through forgiveness, redemption, and resurrection by a great "leap of faith." This theology also emphasized a Christian Realism about society. It stressed the evil not only in human beings but also in human institutions. Yet it also stressed the possibility humans have to transform the world in dependence on the grace of God. Some, however, either saw aspects of Neo-Orthodoxy as liberalism in disguise or as another expression of Fundamentalism.

During those years, some Presbyterians became nationally recognized preachers: The Reverend Clarence E. MacCartney, of the First Presbyterian Church, Pittsburgh; George Buttrick, Madison Avenue Presbyterian Church, New York; John A. Redhead, Jr., of the First Presbyterian Church, Greensboro, North Carolina; Donald G. Barnhouse, Tenth Presbyterian Church, Philadelphia; and Louis H. Evans, First Presbyterian Church, Hollywood. Peter Marshall, of the New York Avenue Presbyterian Church, Washington, D.C., was chaplain to the U.S. Senate. In the Spring of 1947 he prayed with that body:

> Gracious Father, we, Thy children, so often confused, live at cross-purposes in our central aims, and hence we are at cross-purposes with each other. Take us by the hand and help us to see things from Thy viewpoint, that we may see them as they really are. We come to choices and decisions with a prayer upon our lips, for our wisdom fails us. Give us Thine, that we may do Thy will. In Jesus' name. Amen.

James Stewart appeared in "It's a Wonderful Life" (1946), winning the hearts of many for his sermonettes.

Moreover, Presbyterians began to show more concern for the theological education of its ordained leadership. In the PCUSA, for example, as part of a new funding procedure, theological seminaries began to receive a percentage of the church's total benevolence giving. The pattern for PCUS seminaries was more regional. Moreover, a Council of Theological Education was organized in 1943. Under the General Assembly, this council membership included representatives from all seminaries and boards of the church and also from the church at large. The council helped the seminaries cooperate with one another, relating theological education as closely to the church as possible and calling the attention of the churches to the needs of the seminaries. Seminaries experienced a sizeable increase in enrollment, in part because of the war, delayed occupational choices, and the "GI Bill." New journals, *Theology Today* (1946), published by Princeton Theological Seminary, and *Interpretation* (1947), published by Union Theological Seminary in Virginia, represented fresh theological insights.

Presbyterians also realized after the war that they were now actually a part of a global ecumenical community, ecumenical meaning the whole inhabited world. This applied to the human family and also to the emerging Christian family that now circled the earth. This family came together after the war to form the World Council of Churches (WCC), to fulfill Christ's prayer in John 17:21: "That they may all be one." The great missionary conferences, the New York Missionary Conference in New York in 1900 and that in Edinburgh of 1910, represented one stream of flowing toward a world organization to make that oneness manifest and to provide continual contact among Christians. The mission movement formed the International Missionary Council in 1921 to develop global mission strategy. Meanwhile, other streams sprang up. Christians organized "Life and Work" conferences that met first in Stockholm, Sweden, in 1925; another, in Oxford in 1937. There they began to discuss world problems. Christians also gathered for "Faith and Order" meetings, where leaders attempted to deal with Christian differences, both doctrinal and in governance. One of these conferences was held in Lausanne, Switzerland, in 1927; another, in Edinburgh in 1937.

In 1948 the Life and Work and Faith and Order Conferences united to form the WCC, in Amsterdam, Holland, with 150 member churches, Reformed among them. The Reformed Churches in general, and the Presbyterian churches in the United States, were deeply involved in the founding of this organization. Willem Visser't Hooft (1900–1985), of the Dutch Reformed Church in the Netherlands, was the first general secretary of the council. Cavert, Presbyterian executive of the FCC, along with Virginian Francis Pickens Miller (1895–1978), an elder of the PCUS and long involved in the work of the World's Student Christian Federation, played large roles in bringing the WCC into being. Cavert supervised the planning of the first meeting, the theme of which was "God's Design and Man's Disorder." Christians from all over the world, after a turbulent period of history, reaffirmed faith in God and God's gracious purposes for all humankind. The message of the Council is summarized in one of its statements:

> There is a word of God for our world. It is that the world is in the hands of the living God, Whose will for it is wholly good; that in Christ Jesus, His incarnate Word, Who lived and died and rose from the dead, God has broken the power of evil once for all, and opened for every one the gate into freedom and joy in the Holy Spirit; that the final judgment on all human history and on every human deed is the judgment of the merciful Christ; and that the end of history

will be the triumph of His Kingdom, where alone we shall understand how much God has loved the world.

Presbyterians began the twentieth century with a word of love for the world. At mid-century, they joined other Christians in expressing a word of hope for the future.

11

From the Flourishing 1950s to the Frustrating 1970s

During the 1950s and 1960s, Presbyterians were prominent in American life. Editor Henry Luce (1898–1967), the son of Presbyterian missionaries to China, and an elder in the Madison Avenue Presbyterian Church, New York, helped shape the nation's consciousness through *Time, Life, Fortune,* and, later, *Sports Illustrated.* He wrote about the twentieth century as *The American Century* (1940), a time when American would be the Good Samaritan of the world. Dwight David Eisenhower, president of the United States, joined the National Presbyterian Church in Washington, D.C., a church also attended by his secretary of state, John Foster Dulles. Other Presbyterians were members of the cabinet. Eisenhower helped dedicate the headquarters of the new National Council of Churches (NCC), which was organized in 1950 as the successor of the FCC, to consolidate the work of a number of independent Christian agencies under one organization and one roof. In 1954 the World Council of Churches (WCC) held its second plenary meeting in Evanston, Illinois, where delegates from all over the world discussed, "Christ, the Hope of the World." *Time* featured Henry Pitney Van Dusen (1897–1975), president of Union Theological Seminary and prominent theologian-ecumenist, on its front cover in 1954. Eisenhower's stature helped make the 1950s expansive years. He presided over the largest public works project in history, the national security interstate and interurban highway system, and expanded the defense system, which he later called a "military-industrial" complex that influenced everything, even the life of faith. These years paved the way to the frustrations of the 1960s and 1970s.

After victory over the Axis Powers (Germany, Italy, and Japan) in 1945, Presbyterians faced the "cold war" with the Soviet Union. Winston

Churchill, speaking in 1946 at Westminster College, Fulton, Missouri, focused on the "iron curtain" that was descending between the West and the Soviet Union. Churchill's speech defined the situation. The cold war actually began with a hot war in Korea. This war tested the policy of containment of the Soviet Union and the forces of Communism. The conflict led to the reestablishment of a line between South and North Korea that the "superpowers" had drawn after World War II. American Presbyterians supported this limited United Nations action as just, although it left Korea, with its growing Presbyterian population, divided geographically and ideologically.

The war also accentuated American fear of communism. Some Presbyterians attacked the obsessive "McCarthyism," as it was called after Senator Joseph McCarthy of Wisconsin. He exploited the fear by making reckless, unsubstantiated charges of disloyalty against some of America's leading citizens, including its clergy, and religious institutions. In the hysteria, Ike was labeled a communist. In 1953, John A. Mackay (1889–1983), former missionary to Latin America and president of Princeton Theological Seminary, was moderator of the PCUSA. He wrote "A Letter to Presbyterians" about McCarthyism. This letter was approved by the General Council and General Assembly of the PCUSA. In it, Mackay warned against an "exclusive concentration" on the threat of Communism. God still rules over human affairs. Communism, Mackay held, would ultimately self-destruct because of its disbelief and its failure to satisfy the deepest human aspirations. While he warned that there is no absolute security in human life, he believed that the best thing for Christians to do is to champion truth, fulfill the prophetic duty of the church—to do justly and love mercy—while developing a "wise defense" for the nation. Trusting God, Christians should engage with others in dialogue and a quest for the well-being of people all over the world. The "Letter" received worldwide attention as a calm and sensible corrective to the anxiety of the years. However, some Presbyterians perceived even this "Letter" as disloyal. During his ministry Mackay inspired generations of Presbyterians to get off the "balcony" and move to the "road" and new frontiers of faith.

Shortly after this, Scottish immigrant, The Reverend George Dougherty, pastor of the New York Avenue Presbyterian Church in Washington, D.C., preached a sermon in which he suggested that the words "under God" ought to be inserted into the Pledge of Allegiance to the flag of the United States of America. President and Mrs. Eisenhower were in the congregation that day, sitting in the Lincoln pew. The idea caught on and by Flag Day 1954 a new pledge containing those words was repeated in the House of Representatives amid much pomp and circumstance. In the midst of cold war tension, Presbyterians tried to be both faithful to God and loyal to their country. During this same time period, Norman Vincent Peale, pastor of the Marble Collegiate Church, New York, promoted his book *The Power of Positive Thinking* (1952), while Billy Graham, an Associate Reformed Presbyterian of Charlotte, North Carolina, turned Baptist, began his Crusades as well as his rise as a world evangelist.

Church Union, Worship, and Education

Beginning in the early 1950s, the PCUSA, the PCUS, and the UPCNA laid plans for a Presbyterian union. Conversations about such a union had been carried on intermittently since the Civil War. They were resumed in the spirit of times. In 1954, a vote was taken on a union plan. The PCUSA and the UPCNA approved it, but the PCUS voted it down at the presbytery level. It failed to receive the required, but difficult, three-fourths vote. Some observed that the plan was not approved because of the unanimous decision in 1954 by the U.S. Supreme Court to desegregate American public education with all "deliberate speed." Not all Presbyterians were ready for this decision and joined campaigns of "massive resistance" against it. Numerous southern Presbyterians did approve of the decision, however. A majority of commissioners to General Assembly approved a paper attacking racism and calling for desegregation in the same year of the court decision.

In 1958, General Assemblies of the PCUSA and the UPCNA came together in Pittsburgh to celebrate the organization of the United Presbyterian Church in the United States of American (UPCUSA). The union brought together heirs of the Reformation from Scotland and Ireland and other ethnic traditions now represented in the constituency. The new denomination adopted the *Westminster Confession* and the *Larger* and *Shorter Catechisms* as doctrinal standards. It also agreed to write a new confession supported by the 1925 opinion of the UPCNA General Assembly, which had expressed the possible need for new confessional guidance for contemporary Christians. The Reverend Theophilus Mills Taylor, of the UPCNA, was elected moderator of the church, and the Reverend Eugene Carson Blake (1906–1983) became the Stated Clerk of the General Assembly. The denomination also adopted existing worship directories of the churches as well as the forms of Government and Discipline, which were appropriately adjusted to accommodate to the new entity. In 1958 the new denomination reported a membership of

3,159,562, with 11,801 clergy, 9,454 congregations, and 1,932,954 in church school.

Manifesting the ecumenical spirit, the PCUSA, the UPCNA, the PCUS, the Associate Reformed Presbyterians, and the Reformed Church in America published Reformed worship materials. They published *The Hymnbook* (1955), which included a large number of the psalms and hymns for the use of congregational singing, along with responsive readings for public worship. In addition, Presbyterians learned and benefited from the liturgical renewal among Christians during these years. Presbyterians began the long task of writing a new *Directory for the Worship of God,* as preliminary to revising *The Book of Common Worship,* continuing liturgical renewal which began in 1903. This latter volume had been reworked in the 1930s, and finally the PCUS officially recommended it for use in its congregations. A new *Directory* was published in 1960, which focused more on Calvin's view of the central importance of the sacraments. The reading and exposition of the Bible led to the Lord's Supper as the climax of Christian corporate worship. These new aids emphasized the importance of congregational participation in the ministry of worship, at the same time warning against excessive subjectivism and introspection. Although God speaks to human beings elsewhere, it is in public worship that "Jesus Christ in Scripture, sermon, and sacrament confronts" men and women and children and brings them into communion with the divine. Here God provides the believer with nourishment for faith and life. The results of this work were published in *The Book of Common Worship Provisional Series* in 1966, indicative of the ongoing developments in this arena of the church's life. Under the auspices of the UPCUSA and the PCUS and the Cumberland Presbyterian Church, *The Worshipbook: Services and Hymns* was published in 1972.

Some Presbyterians were caught up during this period in the "charismatic" movement, or the "Era of the Spirit," as some called it. In general, those in the Reformed tradition had been suspicious of—if not hostile to—experiences of glossolalia. They believed that speaking in tongues had been confined to the early church. The UPCUSA and PCUS finally acknowledged that persons still had this experience. The divisiveness of the issue motivated the UPCUSA and PCUS to study the biblical, theological, experiential, and ecclesiastical aspects of the movement and to issue reports. In these reports, the churches expressed gratitude for the new spiritual vitality of those who had this experience. At the same time they reminded members that glossolalia was not the chief spiritual gift, that it was not given to or meant for all, and that Presbyterians should avoid divisiveness because of it. These reports echo the mediating approach of the church that had been taken toward the Great Awakening in the 1730s and 1740s. Catherine Marshall (1914–1983), a supporter of the spiritual renewal, added to the popularity of her minister husband through *A Man Called Peter* (1951), which was made into a popular movie. She also contributed to the new spiritual awakening. Many women were inspired by her contributions to *Guideposts*, and her books, including *Beyond Ourselves* (1961) and the autobiographical novel, *Christy* (1967).

After World War II, Presbyterians turned their attention to evangelism and to education as vital to the Christian family. Concerned about growth, the PCUSA began the New Life Movement in 1947, which increased the membership of the church. The Reverend George Sweazey, author of *Effective Evangelism* (1953), headed the effort. Aware of demographic patterns and geographic shifts, Presbyterian denominations followed members and other Americans to the suburbs after the war. Presbyterians built numerous new churches across the landscape with considerable success. The PCUS also took evangelism and church building seriously in its program in 1961, the "Presbyterian Mission to the Nation." Although the main emphasis of the church was placed on the World War II generation, Presbyterians did not neglect completely other populations such as those in the city, in Appalachia, or racial groups such as African Americans.

Furthermore, the denominations developed very demanding educational programs that attempted to deepen Christian maturity. As early as 1948, the PCUSA employed the *Christian Faith and Life* curriculum, which was succeeded by the UPCUSA's *Christian Faith and Action* approach in 1970. The PCUS mounted the *Covenant Life* curriculum in 1963. These curricula provided lessons appropriate for each age. Moreover, they covered a spectrum of Christian studies—for example, about Christ, the Bible, Christian history and theology, and Christian ethics. These curricula were also developed with an ecumenical spirit, calling for considerable participation and cooperation by church staffs, teachers, and those who attended church schools and other church programs. In order to cover church activities, the PCUS published *Presbyterian Survey*, a monthly magazine, and the PCUSA published *Presbyterian Life,* one of the most widely circulated magazines in the country at the time because of its every-member plan. Later the UPCUSA cooperated with the United Church of Christ for a time to publish *A.D.* for their memberships.

Presbyterians also followed their members into higher education, especially veterans of the war now supported by the federal government in what was called the "GI Bill." This complicated the mission of church colleges because of a growing dependence on public funds. By 1956 fifty-two colleges and universities were associated with Presbyterian churches. In the 1950s a Presbyterian College Union coordinated the support of Presbyterians of their institutions, while the Presbyterian Westminster Foundation sponsored work on 144 non-Presbyterian campuses. In 1961 the General Assembly of the UPCUSA adopted a study of "The Church and Higher Education," which reaffirmed church dedication to Christian education, academic excellence, and freedom of inquiry, with a critical and prophetic spirit. These changes would prepare Christian youth for vocations in every area of human thought and life. Over the years, the rules concerning required chapel attendance and required biblical and religious studies were relaxed because of the changing conditions and expectations, including the use of federal funds by church institutions.

World War II increased the awareness of Presbyterians, as well as other Christians, of the fact that the missionary movement of the nineteenth and early twentieth centuries had brought into existence a global Christian community on which the sun never sets. Because Presbyterians through missions had encouraged the organization of self-governing, self-supporting, self-propagating churches, they now faced the process of dealing with the Reformed churches that had developed throughout the world and now asserted independence. Colonial powers had confronted a similar problem which was sometimes violent, when former colonies had asserted their independence. In 1956 the PCUSA held a conference at Lake Mohonk, Pennsylvania, as did the PCUS in 1962 at Montreat, North Carolina, to turn leadership roles over to these new churches. The meetings were attended by representatives of older and newer churches, who helped devise fresh relationships and strategies for mission. The mission field was now defined as the whole world, darkest Europe and America, as well as "darkest Africa," Asia, and Latin America. All members and churches, wherever they are located, were responsible for missions. Missionaries were now "fraternal workers," or "partners in obedience," and they were encouraged to labor with one another and with other Christian bodies. The former sending churches, might be called on for leadership and resources, but they were to explore with the new churches how these contributions should best be employed. The mission conferences were attempts to curb the paternalism and arrogance of the old system and to recognize the new realities of the mission challenge. When the UPCUSA reorganized its missionary work, it did so under a Commission on Ecumenical Mission and Relations (COEMAR), formed as a result of this consultative process. The church decided that everything the churches do is to be a witness to the Gospel of Jesus Christ. Therefore the word mission was used instead of missions to express this insight. This did not satisfy

Presbyterians who did not wish to lose sight of the importance of evangelism.

Gender, Race, Economics, and War

Presbyterians faced large societal challenges during these years, having to do with gender, race, economics, and war. Some critics began to write about the "suburban captivity of the church" and complained about the irresponsible "noise" of its "solemn assemblies." Recognizing this, church leaders, in cooperation with boards and agencies, often developed statements and studies to help Presbyterians understand the larger issues of the times and to stimulate responsible debate and actions among Christians. These materials were "ministerial and declarative," not binding of the conscience, following a provision going back to the first General Assembly in 1789. Some of these studies and statements caused considerable discomfort among some Presbyterians. They did raise the consciousness of members about modern "cases of conscience," to use a phrase from the *Westminster Confession.*

Gender issues came to the forefront after World War II. During the war, and afterward, Presbyterians developed strong women's and men's organizations. A National Council of Women's Organizations emerged in 1943, to become the United Presbyterian Women in 1958. This organization brought women together every four years to consult with one another about their religious responsibilities. A National Council of Presbyterian Men, organized in 1948, encouraged men to participate at every level of church and societal life. This organization became the United Presbyterian Men in 1958. During the war women served in the armed forces, and many began to work outside of the home. This trend continued and, later, both the women and men's organizations began to suffer for lack of participation.

During these years, women became full participants in the ministry of the church: in 1956, the PCUSA voted to ordain women and the Reverend Margaret Towner became the first woman to be ordained to the ministry of Word and Sacrament; in 1964, the PCUS followed suit and ordained the Reverend Rachel Henderlite to that office; in 1972, Mrs. Lois Stair (1923–1981), a businesswoman of Wisconsin, was elected by the UPCUSA to be the first woman moderator of a Presbyterian General Assembly; and in 1978, Mrs. Sarah B. Moseley, a Texan, was elected the first woman moderator of the PCUS. The writings of Presbyterian scholar Letty

M. Russell, including *Human Liberation in a Feminist Perspective* (1974) and *The Liberating Word: A Guide to a Non-Sexist Interpretation of the Bible* (1976), expressed women's aspirations in biblical and theological terms.

Presbyterians also responded to the sexual revolution. The studies of Professor Alfred Kinsey—of Scottish Presbyterian ancestry—on human sexuality in the 1940s and 1950s, the emergence of the "Playboy" and "Playgirl" ethos, and the development of the birth control pill, were factors that revolutionized gender relations. Presbyterian pastoral counselor Seward Hiltner of the University of Chicago, later of Princeton Theological Seminary, published one of the earliest books about the implications of the Kinsey findings. He maintained that whereas Christians had to reject Kinsey's naturalist approach, the churches had to deal with his findings. Presbyterians began to study and then produce papers about responsible sexual behavior becoming to Christians. In this connection, Presbyterians faced the issues of abortion after the Supreme Court decision of *Roe v. Wade* (1972). Presbyterian Warren Burger presided as Chief Justice of the Supreme Court that made that decision. In general, Presbyterians discouraged abortions but judged them permissible under extraordinary circumstances, after the counsel of pastors and physicians. So Presbyterians attempted to find their way through changes in gender and sexual behavior.

In the civil rights movement of the 1950s and 1960s, Presbyterians faced the racism left over from the Civil War. This racism fueled resistance to the Supreme Court decision calling for the desegragation of American education in the North, South, East and West. As early as 1946, the PCUSA adopted for itself the call of the FCC for a "non-segregated church in a non-segregated society," and the PCUSA and PCUS did away with their segregated synods in the 1950s. Presbyterians supported the peaceful protests of persons, such as Martin Luther King, Jr., and his followers. Eugene Carson Blake, Stated Clerk of the UPCUSA, and then president of the NCC, was arrested in Baltimore, Maryland, on July 4, 1963, when he joined other African-American and other white leaders in an attempt to desegregate an amusement park. Although he did not spend time in jail, he did represent much of American Protestantism in his actions. James McBride Dabbs, elder, author, lecturer, and owner of Rip Raps Plantation in South Carolina, tried to explain and open up new possibilities for the South without discrimination and division. He too protested racism. The UPCUSA set up a Commission of Religion and Race (later the Council on Church and Race), whereas the PCUS created the Black Presbyterian Leadership Caucus to help deal with racial and ethnic issues among Presbyterians and in society. Moderator Lois Stair helped the church work through the disruption caused by the UPCUSA's attempt, through one of its agencies, to help avowed Communist Angela Davis obtain a fair trial for alleged complicity in murder. This controversy so disturbed so many members of the church that black Presbyterian leaders voluntarily restored from their own private resources the funds that had been granted to her.

Presbyterians continued to take seriously their responsibility which went back to 1787 and to finally live up to professions of Christian faith and life. In 1964, the Reverend Edler Hawkins (b. 1908) became the first black moderator of the UPCUSA. In 1974, the PCUS elected the Reverend Lawrence Bottoms (b. 1921) to be moderator of its highest governing body. Both Hawkins and Bottoms played key roles in denominational attempts to deal with racism. This black self-consciousness stimulated what became known as *liberation theology,* based on the themes of the deliverance of the children of Israel from the land of bondage of Egypt and the clear message of Jesus that Christians should minister to the least, the last, and the lost of this world. With his studies, *Black Religion and Black Radicalism* (1972) and *Black and Presbyterian: The Heritage and Hope* (1980), the Reverend Gayraud Wilmore (b. 1921) became a leading black theologian. The Reverend J. Oscar McCloud (b. 1936) served the UPCUSA as general director of its Program Agency. Presbyterians were enriched as women, Native-American, Hispanic-American, African-American, and Asian-American authors and artists expressed in feminine, racial, and ethnic terms how Jesus identified with the human situation in incarnational terms. Some critics, however, were concerned when God was referred to as feminine, and Jesus as red, yellow, and black.

American Presbyterians, along with Christians of other denominations, gave attention to economic problems and poverty in a land of affluence and plenty. These concerns can be traced from the days of Calvin in Geneva to the days of the Depression of the 1930s when Christians tried to deal with economic conditions. Under the supervision of Presbyterian Cameron Hall and with the aid of laity such as Dean Rusk of the Rockefeller Foundation, the NCC conducted an extended study from 1949–1965 on "Ethics and Economic Life." The study recognized how America had evolved as a nation with a mixed economy. It also explored how it could be made more just, nationally and internationally, for owners, employers and employees, the young, the middle-aged, and the elderly. In a study, *The Church, the Christian, and Work* (1967), Presbyterians, long known for their work ethic, also stressed the need for meaningful labor for all. They grew more conscious of poverty, of the "other

America," often invisible to travelers on interstate highways over urban squalor, through Appalachian mountains, and across southwestern deserts. The PCUSA and the PCUS urged members to seek a more equitable distribution of wealth for the poor, and also for the health of the whole social and political system. Concerned about the growing disparity between the rich and the poor, Presbyterians in the 1960s joined other Christians in encouraging the "war on poverty." Furthermore, the Presbyterian denominations became more sensitive to environmental problems. Presbyterians emphasized in their public statements the stewardship of the environment, thus showing concern for posterity as well as for natural resources.

Presbyterian denominations also gave attention to matters of war and peace. They began to live with—if not to love—the nuclear weapons. In the 1950s, as the cold war heated up and nuclear arms grew more and more powerful, churches expressed concern over the spread and the possible use of these weapons, encouraging means of control. Whereas Presbyterians accepted the Korean War as just and necessary, they were divided over the Vietnam War as it escalated under successive presidents. Presbyterians such as Secretary of State Dean Rusk and Secretary of Defense Robert McNamara, for example, helped set policy and manage the war in Southeast Asia. They were opposed by many, including both Presbyterian clergy and laity, some with national followings, and especially among the youth. Stanford University Professor Robert McAfee Brown, Yale Chaplain William Sloane Coffin, and Oberlin College ethicist Edward T. Long, Jr., who wrote *War and Conscience in America* (1968), offered leadership to the antiwar movement. While starting out with the assumption that the war in Southeast Asia was a legitimate part of America's containment policy, some Presbyterians in the UPCUSA and PCUS began to confess confusion over the purposes of the war. They also began to question the way the counterinsurgery was being fought. They raised questions as to whether the war in Vietnam was just and necessary. When the United States invaded Cambodia, the UPCUSA expressed official objections, whereas the PCUS addressed a series of respectful inquiries to American authorities about the purposes and methods used in the war. When the war finally grinded to a halt, the nation as well as the religious communities breathed a sigh of relief. Americans, however, remained deeply divided. Presbyterians turned their attention to "the nation's wounds," to use Lincoln's words. In discussing the arms race carried on worldwide, Presbyterians called for restraint but remained divided over these issues.

The Confession of 1967

Since the mid-nineteenth century, some members had been calling for fresh statements expressing what Presbyterians believed about God and human nature and destiny. The PCUSA amended the *Westminster Confession* in 1903 and produced a Brief Statement of the Reformed Faith, as the UPCNA did in 1925. The PCUS also produced another Brief Statement in 1962. In the 1960s the UPCUSA engaged in the adoption and writing of a *Book of Confessions,* containing a contemporary *Confession of 1967.* Members were not of one heart of mind. Some were known as "private Christians," interested in personal conversion and conduct; others, known as "public Christians," interested in societal problems and the conversion of social institutions. Actually, these categories oversimplified Presbyterian concerns. The confessional committee headed by Professor Edward Dowey of Princeton Theological Seminary, which was appointed to draw up a new statement of faith, decided to focus on the theme of reconciliation. First, it identified itself with the larger Christian and Reformed family by proposing a book that included the "Apostles' Creed," the "Nicene Creed," the *Scots Confession,* the *Heidelberg Catechism,* the *Second Helvetic Confession,* the *Westminster Confession* and the *Shorter Catechism,* and the *Theological Declaration of Barmen* (1934) from the German Confessing Church. In the face of Naziism and other modern nationalist idolatries, this last doctrine stressed the earliest Christian confession: "Jesus Christ is Lord."

Second, the committee proposed the new *Confession of 1967,* so-called to emphasize the confessing as well as a confessional nature of the church. The committee based the statement on fundamental biblical promise: "in Christ God was reconciling the world to himself" (2 Cor. 5:19), with verses 17–21 as a whole emphasizing God's relationship to us and our relationship to one another. The new confession was trinitarian, but treated the Son, Father, and Spirit in the order of the Apostolic Benediction. It did not use all of the technical language of the Hellenic creeds, and was christocentric, beginning with the "eternal Son of the Father" who makes God known through the work of reconciliation. Christ is God's Word, to whom the Bible, as God's Word written, points, and which Christians should study with all the critical means possible to better understand the Gospel. Christ's work as Redeemer is confessed and described, using the biblical references to Christ as a reconciler, ransom, substitutionary atonement, supreme pattern for life, and underscoring the richness of the biblical imagery. Christ exposes as well as redeems from the self-interest and hostility that infects all human authority and attitudes, however virtuous.

God shows love as Creator as well as Redeemer. The world and human beings, male and female, "reflect to the eye of faith the majesty and mystery" of the Creator. This world of time and space is the sphere of God's dealing with human beings in all "its beauty and vastness, sublimity and awfulness, order and disorder." God as Spirit "gathers" Christians into the church to praise God, and then sends them into the world to serve God in a variety of callings. Christians are equipped through worship, prayer, the interpretation of the Word, and the sacraments. God's redeeming work in Jesus Christ "embraces the whole of man's life: social and cultural, economic and political, scientific and technological, individual and corporate." The committee chose to focus special attention on the call to reconciliation in family relations and in the areas of race, economics, and war, enduring as well as contemporary challenges. The *Confession of 1967* affirmed the resurrection of Jesus Christ as "God's sign that he will consummate his work of creation and reconciliation beyond death and bring to fulfillment the new life begun in Christ." Thus God transcends as well as identifies with humans in the life, death, and resurrection of Jesus Christ. It should be noted that in the confession, Presbyterians respectfully recognized the other religions of the world that Christians are called on to understand, and with whose adherents we are to share the message of Christ's reconciliation of all to God.

Members of the UPCUSA—as well as Presbyterians in other denominations—debated the merits of the new proposal for two years. At the same time, the General Assembly and the presbyteries debated the adoption of two new ordination questions. The first was "Do you accept the Scriptures of the Old and New Testaments to be the unique and authoritative witness to Jesus Christ in the Church catholic and by the Holy Spirit God's Word to you?" The second was "Will you perform the duties of a minister [to be changed to cover other officers] in obedience to Jesus Christ, the authority of the Scriptures and under the continuing guidance of the confessions of this Church?" Some Presbyterians were very vocal in their opposition to the *Book of Confessions* with its "Confession of 1967." They fought it as unbiblical, and carried on a public ad campaign in leading newspapers to defeat it. It was approved, however, by 82 percent of all the presbyteries, as well as by the General Assembly. When the final affirmative vote was reported, the General Assembly rose to sing "Praise God from Whom all Blessings Flow." Thus the UPCUSA embraced the Christian, Reformed, and Presbyterian traditions with its new *Confession of*

1967 as a confessional and confessing church, seeking thereby the peace, unity, and purity in a new period in the life of the church.

Later in the 1970s the PCUS also produced a *Book of Confessions* and a new *Declaration of Faith,* under the leadership of the Reverend Dr. Albert C. Winn. This was longer than the new UPCUSA confession and written in more liturgical language for use in worship. In 1977 the PCUS presbyteries narrowly defeated this attempt to adopt a new confessional standard. The *Declaration,* however, was widely admired and used liturgically as an affirmation of Christian faith. The PCUS dealt in this confessional statement with the ethical demands of those years. The Reverend Aubrey N. Brown, Jr. (b. 1908), editor of the *Presbyterian Outlook* of Richmond, Virginia, supported these efforts at confessional revision, together with other progressive movements among all Presbyterians. In 1970 the *Outlook,* heir of independent Presbyterian journalism, celebrated its 150th anniversary as it continued to serve the ecumenical interests of the PCUS and the UPCUSA. The *Southern Presbyterian Journal,* published in North Carolina, opposed these new confessional developments. Other Presbyterians began to publish the *Presbyterian Layman* and *reNew* for Presbyterians for Renewal, to provide conservative perspectives on denominational faith and life.

Ministry, Reorganization, and Ecumenics

In the decades following World War II, Presbyterians gave attention to the laity and the ministry in the church, engaged in a reorganization of the agencies of the denomination, and embarked on new ecumenical endeavors. America became a highly mobile, pan-urban society with decaying cities and with sprawling suburbs, into which more and more Presbyterians moved. Some continued, however, to make their living in the urban centers. With these changing demographic patterns, ecclesiastical boundaries did not always facilitate efficient and effective witness. Americans became more and more detached from one another as a people. Presbyterians placed an emphasis on an interrelated and interacting global society.

Between 1958 and 1972, the UPCUSA, produced a report titled *The Church and Its Changing Ministry.* These studies included laity and their mission in the church and in the world. Presbyterians reemphasized the universal priesthood and prophethood of all believers, the importance of laity as well as clergy in the life of the church and the world. The laity were encouraged to serve God in their vocations and daily jobs, as well as through their work in a local congregation. Presbyterians also had to deal with the numerous special ministries and specialties for which clergy began to be trained, including callings as pastoral counselors, chaplains in prisons, hospitals, and the armed forces, and church administrators. In this connection, under the guidance of such persons as Presbyterian-Congregationalist minister Anton Boisen in *The Exploration of the Inner World* (1937) and Seward Hiltner in his writings, including *Preface to Pastoral Theology* (1958), pastoral care became an essential part of the training of church leadership. Physician Karl Menninger, an elder and a Presbyterian Sunday school teacher in Topeka, Kansas, contributed to this movement and, with his reflections on *Whatever Became of Sin?* (1972), called for a greater sense of responsibility in modern life. This development threatened to throw the balance of clergy and laity in church governing bodies out of balance. Reaffirming the parity of all believers, congregations were granted additional lay representatives in government bodies in proportion to congregational membership. Ministerial relations committees of presbyteries began to play a larger role in the placement of candidates for the ministry, although Presbyterians still insisted on the right of each congregation to select its own minister. In this period, the "pastor-director" tended to replace the "preacher-teacher" model for ministry, emphasizing the important function of the clergy in helping all parishioners to do the work of ministry.

Because of the changing demography of the country, Presbyterians also went through a major process of reorganization, something they had not done since the 1920s. Some Presbyterians grew disenchanted with the centralized organizations that had been effective in the past, especially immediately after World War II. The UPCUSA attempted to steer between localism and the concentration of church power and authority. It tried to make the governing bodies work more responsibly for the good of the congregations as well as the good of the whole church doing work in national and global mission.

In 1969, the General Council reorganized as the General Assembly Mission Council, subject to the General Assembly. It had the responsibility of dealing with the overlapping and the rivalry among the various agencies. The functions of the previous boards were consolidated and coordinated in a Program Agency, which did away with the overlapping and competition. The Support Agency was created to integrate financial and promotional programs with interpretation and stewardship development, while the Vocation Agency helped serve the ever-changing roles of the clergy and laity in the denomination. The larger synods of the church were given more representatives on these agencies than smaller bodies. In the UPCUSA, a special committee on synod boundaries organized fifteen regional synods, preserving state boundaries while doing so, pushing synods to extend responsibilities in the areas of Programs, Support, and Vocations. The PCUS went through similar discussions and decisions to make the mission of the church more responsive to contemporary challenges. Although the intentions were good, some critics thought the plans lost focus on specific tasks that had been represented by the former boards and agencies, no matter how businesslike in theory the new plan seemed to be.

Presbyterians divided and also engaged in new ecumenical ventures during this period. Unfortunately, in 1973, some congregations withdrew from the PCUS to form the Presbyterian Church in America because of their concerns regarding such issues as the ordination of women to the ministry and the new confessional standards. Robert McAfee Brown, who sometimes wrote under the pen name St. Hereticus, came up with this parody of "Onward Christian Soldiers" to expose divisiveness and to encourage ecumenical relations:

> Like a fleeing army
> Moves the Church of God;
> Brother treads on brother,
> Grinds him in the sod.
>
> We are not united,
> Lots of bodies we:
> One lacks faith, another hope,
> And all lack charity.
>
> Backward, Christian soldiers,
> Waging fruitless wars,
> Breaking out in schisms
> That our God deplores.

The PCUS and the UPCUSA continued to express interest in union. In 1969, the two denominations allowed some individual presbyteries to belong simultaneously to the PCUS and UPCUSA, forming union presbyteries and thus bringing Presbyterians together, especially in the border regions along the Mason-Dixon line. Moreover, the two denominations decided to meet in General Assemblies in the same city at the same time in alternate years to increase familiarity with one another. The PCUS, the UPCUSA, and the CPC continued relations with the World Alliance of Reformed Churches (Presbyterian and Congregationalist), so renamed after the Alliance united with the International Congregational Council in 1970. The Alliance, with headquarters in Geneva, now involved Reformed bodies from all over the world, as well as Europe and the United States.

In a nationally celebrated sermon of 1960, Blake of the UPCUSA proposed that the Protestant Episcopal Church, the United Church of Christ, the United Methodist Church, and Presbyterian Churches, along with others, establish a united church that would be truly Catholic, truly Reformed, and truly Evangelical. These churches, including the UPCUSA, the PCUS, and the CPC, joined together in "The Consultation on Church Union," known later as the "Church of Christ Uniting." COCU, as it was known, represented a desire at one level and in a new period, to put aside the divisions in the body of Christ that had occurred during the sixteenth, seventeenth, and eighteenth centuries in the British Isles, as well as some divisions that had occurred since among Christians. A "Plan of Union" proposed to provide for the recognition of the congregational, presbyterian, and episcopal aspects of church government as they are found in the Scriptures. The participating denominations shared much in common and grew together. Boundaries between denominations were disappearing gradually. For example, the Presbyterian and Congregational systems over the years developed executive officers whose responsibilities are sometimes similar to those of bishops.

The most important breakthroughs in Christian relations in this period were between Protestants and Roman Catholics and Orthodox Christians. Orthodox Christians became members of the WCC and the NCC. In the 1950s Eugene Carson Blake, as president of the NCC, helped organize exchange visits between Protestant church leaders in the United States and Russian Orthodox churchmen. These visits and conversations deescalated the ideological conflict between East and West. After Vatican Council II, Roman Catholics and Presbyterians, recognizing one another as separated brothers and sisters, developed warmer relations. Presbyterian scholars Robert McAfee Brown and James Hastings Nichols of the University of Chicago, later of Princeton Theological Seminary, were, among others, participant-observers at the historic Second Vatican Council meetings in the 1960s. When Blake was called to be the secretary general of the WCC in Geneva, he welcomed the Greek Orthodox patriarch to Geneva with a fraternal kiss. He also greeted Paul VI, who became the first pope to visit the Reformation city in over four hundred years. Presbyterians gave thanks to God for these expressions of Christian unity and for an ecumenical paper, *Baptism, Eucharist, and Ministry* (1982). This paper, which was produced at the WCC, described the Presbyterian agreement, and, in some cases, disagreement, with these other communions in matters of worship.

12

Reunion, Renewal, and Global Responsibilities

When John Glenn, Presbyterian graduate of Muskingum College, circled the globe in a space craft, he dramatized the reality that this world is one world. When Neil A. Armstrong and Edwin E. Aldrin set foot on the lunar surface, late in 1969, they lifted the spirits of all people everywhere. Aldrin, a Presbyterian elder, reminded all of God the Creator, Redeemer, and Sustainer, when he stowed a small amount of bread and wine on the space module to celebrate a lunar communion. This remarkable lunar walk hid only for a moment the numerous difficulties we faced in those years, including a continuous cold war between the United States and the Soviet Union, and their various allies. Toward the end of the 1980s, the cold war seemed to terminate with the dissolution of the Soviet Union. This event was celebrated with the destruction of the Berlin Wall. It also uncovered numerous problems, including questions about what the cold war had done to American society.

During the 1970s and 1980s, Presbyterians also took part in the observances of the 200th anniversaries of the American Revolution (1976) and the writing and ratification of the Constitution of the United States of America (1989), in which the Reformed had participated. They also celebrated the 200th anniversary of the first General Assembly in 1989. Two hundred years earlier, the Reverend Jedediah Chapman, moderator of the Synod of New York and Philadelphia in 1788, preached a sermon calling for Presbyterian cooperation and unity on the text, Eph. 4:3–4, urging Christians to keep "the unity of the Spirit in the bond of peace." At the first meeting of the General Assembly in 1789, the aging John Witherspoon had expressed concern for a dependence on God for the well-being and growth of the church. He preached on the text of 1 Cor. 3:7:

"So neither he who plants nor he who waters is anything, but only God gives the growth" (KJV). Two hundred years later, Presbyterians faced the testing of their identity, unity, and purposes as a family of God's people. They heard calls to renewal at all levels of Christian faith and life and to their responsibilities in the world.

Changing Influence and Demographics

During these decades, Protestants in general have had to wrestle with the meaning of what some call a cultural "disestablishment" (after the legal disestablishment of the eighteenth century). This meant that so-called Mainline or Oldline Protestants, including Presbyterians, did not wield the influence that they once did in American faith and life. Critics called them "Sidelined" Protestants. Protestants have had to share the American stage with Roman Catholicism, Orthodoxy, Judaism, and other religious groups, for example, television evangelists and their followers, who grew more influential in public life. During these years, there was considerable "WASP swatting," as white, Anglo-Saxon, Protestants were accused of being responsible for many of the social ills that beset the nation and the world. WASPS were not easy on WASPS, recognizing truths in these criticisms. Some observers suggested, in a twist of the point, that other religious communities have been, to an extent, "protestantized." For example, Protestants and Roman Catholics have grown more alike. They read a common Bible and shared liturgical, theological, and ethical insights with one another. Despite papal prohibitions, Protestant and Roman Catholics occasionally joined one another at the Lord's Table. Moreover, the pope's unruly American flock, as it was called, pressed for more democracy in the church's life and for married and women priests. Catholics used birth control pills, which a Catholic physician helped to develop. Facing common problems in the nation and the world, many Christians drew closer—moderating the differences of the Reformation. Although Protestants have wielded enormous influence through the years, they have learned to share authority and power with members of other religious groups in America.

Presbyterians have been a minority denominational body since the early nineteenth century. But, even in the latter part of the twentieth century, Presbyterians enjoyed influence out of proportion to their number: the Reverend Claire Randall, graduate of the Presbyterian School of Christian Education, presided over the National Council of Churches (NCC) for a time and was the first NCC official to visit the Peoples Republic of China in 1981 to build bridges to the surviving and growing Christian community there; Sam and Helen Walton of Bentonsville, Arizona, became the nation's retailers via Walmart, and Helen presided over the Presbyterian Foundation for a time; Hugh McColl of Charlotte, North Carolina, became one of the nation's great financial managers with the expansion of Nations Bank; John Templeton became one of the nation's brokers, and established the prestigious Templeton Prize for Religion; the Reverend Richard Halverson of the Fourth Presbyterian Church, Washington, D.C., served as chaplain of the Senate of the United States; Warren Burger, a Presbyterian, presided as Chief Justice of the Supreme Court during those years; Surgeon General C. Everett Koop served as the nation's physician, while John Frohnmayer presided over the National Endowment for the Arts for a time; and the Reverend Frederick Beuchner inspired American clergy and laity with both his theological and fictional writings. At another level, Fred Rogers of *Mr. Rogers' Neighborhood*, and Catherine Patterson, Presbyterian missionary turned author, shaped and challenged American children with their programs and stories; and Ronald Reagan, a member of Alexander Campbell's Disciples of Christ, attended the Belle Aire Presbyterian Church in California with his wife Nancy, who was a member. He served two terms as the nation's president, and reminded citizens that America is still a "city on a hill." Ross Perot, of the Highland Park Presbyterian Church, Dallas, gave voice to the nation's discontent. Despite this influence, the new configurations of American life led to Presbyterian self-evaluation.

Demographic studies, including loss of membership, also caused considerable soul-searching. Between 1966 and 1988, the UPCUSA and the PCUS lost a total of 1,310,935 members, or 30.8 percent of total communicants. Other Christian denominations lost membership also. Some observers suggested that this was because several denominations, including Presbyterians, had neglected the spiritual nurture of congregants, placing too much emphasis on social reform. Although some may have left Presbyterian denominations because of positions on political, economic, and social issues, the situation was more complicated than that. For example, the Presbyterian church grew older. One quarter of its membership in 1988–1990 was sixty-five years or older, causing a considerable loss through death. Because of this trend, the denomination began to give attention to America's aging population. Studies focused on "The Rights and Responsibilities of Older Persons" (1979) and "Older Adult Ministry: Growing in the Abundant Life" (1992). Presbyterian educator, Margaret (Maggie) Kuhn founded and personified the Gray Panthers.

With regard to children, Presbyterian birthrates fell. Presbyterians found it more difficult to hold on to their young people, especially those with higher education. The young, raised with ecumenical sympathies, explored other religious options for themselves, often dropped out of church altogether. Leaders of the churches tried to reverse this loss with evangelism, new church development, and programs to meet the needs of contemporary seekers. In 1985 Presbyterians mounted a program, "New Day Dawning," to introduce people to "the Kingdom of God through repentance and faith in Jesus Christ, and to full participation in the community of faith as an expression of the Kingdom of God."

In the 1980s a group of scholars, directed by John Mulder, Louis B. Weeks, and Milton J. Coalter of Louisville Theological Seminary, produced a seven-volume collection of essays titled *The Presbyterian Presence: The Twentieth-Century Experience* published by Westminster John Knox Press and supported by the Lilly Foundation. It was the most thorough study of any American denomination in recent years. In the final volume, *The Re-forming Tradition: Presbyterians and Mainstream Protestantism* (1992), these scholars concluded that Presbyterians needed to recover a theological vision and to revitalize a nurturing and evangelistic community open to growth. In citing the *Book of Order*, they also warned against human tendency to "idolatry and tyranny" and the need for Presbyterians, with other Christians, to seek justice in the transformation of society. This is what Presbyterians tried to do in an agenda for these years.

Healing and Restructuring

In 1983, Presbyterians in the UPCUSA and the PCUS took an important step to overcome the Civil War past. In the 1970s, concerned for the scandal of division and to manifest the unity of the body of Christ, the denominations appointed a Joint Committee on Presbyterian Union to renew efforts to heal the split. The Reverend Robert C. Lamar and the Reverend J. Randolph Taylor co-chaired the committee. It was made up of equal members from the UPCUSA and the PCUS, representative of minorities and other interests. In the negotiations, the Committee attempted to satisfy those who had biblical, evangelical, and spiritual concerns, as well as those who wished to protect the rights of women and minorities in the church organization. The Committee presented *The Plan of Reunion* to the two General Assemblies in 1981, and in 1982, both bodies adopted the plan and sent it to the presbyteries. All the UPCUSA presbyteries voted positively as did three-fourths of the PCUS presbyteries, thus approving the plan. But 20 percent of those voting in presbyteries and eight presbyteries in the PCUS, including five in South Carolina, voted against the plan, thus indicating some resistance to it.

The General Assemblies meeting in Atlanta, Georgia, in 1983, finally approved the plan. The new General Assembly elected Taylor, born in China, a civil rights leader, and pastor of the Myers Park Presbyterian Church, Charlotte, North Carolina, moderator of the new Presbyterian Church (U.S.A.). As his first act, he led the new denomination in grateful worship to God. Some congregations, for example, those that did not approve of the ordination of women, used a provision provided in the agreement to withdraw from the denomination. The churches began using joint statistics for 1982. The UPCUSA brought into the union 2,351,119 members; 8,975 churches; 15,178 clergy; 87,874 elders; and 811,997 church school members, whereas the PCUS numbered 821,008 members; 4,250 churches; 6,077 clergy; 34,878 elders; and 375,256 church school members.

During and after union discussions, Presbyterians gave much attention to governance. In the process, the new denomination moved the headquarters of the General Assembly and agencies—after some debate—out of New York, Philadelphia, and Atlanta to Louisville, Kentucky, and into a new building on Witherspoon Street. The "Articles of Agreement" provided Presbyterians with a process of growing together governmentally, liturgically, theologically, and programmatically. The new denomination needed new structures for the church. It began to amend the *Book of Order* to meet its needs. In studies titled "Historic Principles, Conscience, and Church Government" (1983) and the "Confessional Nature of the Church" (1988), it reviewed the past "Preliminary Principles" of 1788 and the theological roots of church structures. It confessed that church governance should have a biblical and theological base. After reaffirming that God is Lord of the conscience in ecclesiastical as well as civil affairs, the denomination underscored values in Presbyterian governance for Christian faith and life. In order to relate the parts of the church to the whole, the denomination redrew lines of presbyteries and synods to decentralize, although still emphasizing the work of the General Assembly and its ministry units. It still wrestled with how to make the ministry units of various governing bodies responsible and accountable to the General Assembly and the synods and presbyteries. In order to preserve the representative character of governing bodies, the church tried to devise ways for men, women, youth, and various racial and ethnic groups to serve on the organization's committees at various levels. In studies on ordination, the church stressed the commission and mission of all baptized Christians, as well as the special functions of ordained leaders. Some members in the denomination were suspicious of ecclesiastical bureaucracies, just as many in the society questioned political bureaucrats that appear unresponsive to constituency concerns.

In 1988, Presbyterians prepared another study titled "Is Christ Divided?" This emphasized the variety of God's gifts and the need to value different experiences and expressions of Christian faith, hope, and love in order to remain together for the sake of the Presbyterian family and the whole Christian community. The denomination communicated with its members through *Presbyterian Survey,* which changed its name to *Presbyterians Today,* and *The News,* as well as through synod newspapers. In the reorganization process, the Westminster Press and John Knox Press united and became the Presbyterian Publishing Corporation in Louisville. The Presbyterian Board of Pensions, however, remained in Philadelphia. The Presbyterian Church (U.S.A.) Foundation, with funds from the Trustees of the General Assembly as far back as 1789, moved to Jeffersonville, Indiana. It carried with it, from the UPCUSA and PCUS, assets of approximately $800 million in 1987. It continued to encourage Christian generosity. Although Presbyterian giving to the life and work of congregations and presbytery causes remained high, contributions at the General Assembly level dropped. Leaders at the highest level of the church tried to increase support of denominational programs with designated giving. As in years past, Presbyterians defined stewardship in terms of responsible life and vocation, as well as the use of financial resources. The Historical Foundation in Montreat, North Carolina, founded in 1927, united with the older Presbyterian Historical Society in Philadelphia. The Society continued to serve as the Department of History of the General Assembly of the PC(U.S.A.) with repositories in two locations. It managed the denomination's records and continued to publish *American Presbyterians: Journal of Presbyterian History* founded in 1901.

Worship, Education, and Mission

In churchwide consultations during the anniversary year of 1989, members of the PC(U.S.A.), beginning a new century of ecclesiastical life together, considered what it meant to be a "covenant" people. In addition to governance issues, the denomination continued to give attention to worship, theological reflection, and mission. In the case of worship, the denomination produced rich resources, based on the Reformed tradition, other Christian traditions, and contemporary experience. A new *Directory for the Service of God* was published in 1988 as counsel for clergy and laity.

The directory discussed the dynamics, elements, and orders for Christian worship in various circumstances, including worship in private, in families, and in ministry in the world. It held that:

> Christian worship joyfully ascribes all praise and honor, glory and power to the triune God. In worship the people of God acknowledge God present in the world and their lives. As they respond to God's claim and redemptive action in Jesus Christ, believers are transformed and renewed. In worship the faithful offer themselves to God and are equipped for God's service in the world.

The *Directory* called for more lay participation in worship and its leadership. In this connection, the denomination admitted baptized children—with parental counsel about the significance of such participation—to the Lord's Supper before confirmation. A committee, with a staff headed by Harold M. Daniels of the Theology and Worship Ministry Unit, produced a new *Book of Common Worship* (1993) in cooperation with the CPC. This volume, published by Westminster/John Knox Press, was a rich liturgical resource drawn from the Reformed tradition, the whole body of Christ, and new concerns of Christian worship in the contemporary world. In 1990, Westminster/John Knox Press also published the *Presbyterian Hymnal: Hymns, Psalms, and Spiritual Songs*. Chaired by Melva W. Costen, professor of music at Johnson C. Smith Theological Seminary in Atlanta, the hymnbook committee divided the book into four sections covering the church year, the psalms, hymns on various topics, and service music for various worship occasions. The contributions of Presbyterians to hymnody—for example, writers such as Brian Wren, Professor Thomas H. Traeger and the Reverend Frederick Anderson, and musicians John Weaver and Helen Wright— suggested that the music, in the spirit of David, God's psalmist, was still very much alive among Presbyterians. The *Hymnal* contained Native-American, African-American, Latin-American, and Asian hymns, as well as the inclusive-language hymns of Jane Parker Huber. The denomination encouraged members in the use of these aids in family worship, and it reminded the faithful that keeping the Sabbath is a witness to God's lordship over all life and all time and space.

When the PC(U.S.A.) was constituted in 1983, the denomination adopted a *Book of Confessions*, now including the Apostles' Creed, the Nicene Creed, the *Second Helvetic Confession*, the *Scots Confession*, the *Heidelberg Catechism*, the *Westminster Confession of Faith*, with both the *Larger* and *Shorter Catechisms*, the *Theological Declaration of Barmen*, and *Confession of 1967*. In addition, "A Brief Statement of Belief of the Presbyterian Church in the United States" (1962) was included in the book as a summary of the Reformed understanding of the historic Christian faith and life as set forth in the Bible. Some Presbyterians offered the *Declaration of Faith of 1977* for adoption by the church. The General Assembly recommended its continued study and use but did not adopt it officially. In the meantime, the church continued the faith's pilgrimage as a confessional and confessing church.

In denominational reports on "Biblical Authority and Interpretation" (1982) and "Presbyterian Understanding and Use of Holy Scripture" (1983), Presbyterians examined the place of the Bible in the faith and life of Presbyterians. These studies encouraged Presbyterians to reaffirm the Bible as the "rule of faith and life," and offered guidelines for a believing, loving, and critical study and use under the guidance of the Holy Spirit. The studies observed that the Bible, a bestseller, was not widely studied. The *Women's Bible Commentary* (1992), published by Westminster/John Knox Press, demonstrated the scholarly maturity and insights of women biblical scholars. Another report, "Nature of Revelation in the Christian Tradition from a Reformed Perspective" (1987), encouraged Presbyterians to consider God's self-disclosure as a source and content of revelation, as a matter of faith experience, and as a rational process that may involve "propositional statements" about God and our nature and destiny. The PC(U.S.A.) also considered and adopted in 1991, as a part of the 1983 agreement, a "Brief Statement of Faith" to be used as a whole or in part in worship. It was Christian, trinitarian, Reformed, and inclusive, confessing belief in God in biblical terms. God is

> Like a mother who will not forsake her nursing child,
> like a father who runs to welcome the prodigal home,
> God is faithful still.

Persons such as Howard L. Rice, professor of San Francisco Theological Seminary and former moderator of the denomination, called for a return to and revitalization of what he called *Reformed Spirituality* (1991) in its personal and corporate dimensions. Thus Presbyterians at various levels of the church discussed serious theological problems of Christian faith and life.

However, some observers deplored a weakening of a supportive Christian ethos that might help members of the church benefit from these reflections on and affirmations of faith. As already indicated, the denomination attempted to strengthen worship, thereby putting first things first. In addition, it attempted to strengthen its educational ecology. First, it once again emphasized education for all citizens of the nation by calling for the "Renewal of Public Education" (1987) and by calling Presbyterians to support such renewal. Second, it emphasized congregational nurture and education for children, adults, and for older adults. In the 1970s and 1980s, the church promoted *Christian Education: Shared Approaches,* focusing on "Knowing the Word, Interpreting the Word, Living the Word, and Doing the Word." The Presbyterian and Reformed Educational Ministry (PREM) continued these early efforts with a more user-friendly curriculum for teachers and students. Congregations, however, often explored their own educational options.

The denomination attempted to strengthen ties to the sixty-eight colleges and universities that still claimed association with the PC(U.S.A.), from Hampden-Sydney College (1776) to the Hawaii Loa College established in 1963. The report, *Faith, Knowledge, and the Future—Presbyterian Mission in Higher Education* (1982), explored the importance of higher education for building up the whole Christian family, as well as for exploring life's options. Moreover, the denomination called for strengthening Presbyterian seminaries, encouraging each seminary to make its own special contribution to training the church's leadership, both female and male. The denomination had eleven theological institutions: Princeton Theological Seminary, Union Theological Seminary in Virginia, Auburn Theological Seminary in New York, Pittsburgh Theological Seminary, Columbia Theological Seminary in Georgia, Dubuque Theological Seminary in Iowa, Johnson C. Smith Theological Seminary in Atlanta, McCormick Theological Seminary in Chicago, Austin Theological Seminary, San Francisco Theological Seminary, and the Presbyterian School of Christian Education in Richmond. The Erskine Theological Seminary in Due West, South Carolina, served the Associate Reformed Presbyterian Church, as the Memphis Theological Seminary served the CPC. These institutions trained a growing number of women and second-career candidates for the ministry. A number of candidates also attended university divinity schools, or other institutions such as Gordon-Conwell in New England or Fuller Theological Seminary in Pasadena. A report emphasized the continued need of the church for a committed, educated, pastorally oriented ministry, with practical sense about church administration. President James J. McCord greatly increased the endowment of Princeton Theological Seminary and founded the Center of Theological Inquiry, for advanced reflection on the challenges to Christianity in the world.

In addition to stressing education, which is a very Presbyterian thing to do, Presbyterians emphasized both evangelism and mission. As indicated earlier, the denomination adopted a program of evangelism—"New Day

Dawning." The program explored the contextual nature of evangelism, the possibility as well as the importance of Presbyterian growth, and the need to nurture new members in the faith. The Global Mission Unit continued to strengthen PC(U.S.A.) connections with churches in 56 different countries in 1988, supporting at that time 557 people in global mission. These individuals served ministries in cooperation with Reformed communities in various lands. Presbyterian leaders from sister churches around the world helped enrich Presbyterian witness in America. The denomination's mission agency entered into creative covenant relations with such voluntary agencies as the Medical Benevolence Foundation (Houston, TX), the Presbyterian Frontier Fellowship (Portland, OR), and the Outreach Foundation (Nashville, TN) to encourage cross-cultural mission. Meanwhile, the 100th edition of the *Mission Yearbook for Prayer and Study* proclaimed, in 1992, "Jesus Christ as universal sovereign" of the entire planet.

The presence in the United States of thousands of Asian immigrants was a result of Presbyterian mission and of a promise of mission in the future. The National Asian Presbyterian Council was organized in 1972. Koreans, however, presented a special challenge in America. About 70 percent of the Protestants in Korea at that time were in Presbyterian churches. In the 1980s, from 700,000 to 1,000,000 Koreans immigrated to the United States. During those years they became members of numerous denominations, including the PC(U.S.A.). The Koreans found themselves in a transition between cultures, sometimes marginalized and treated paternalistically by the Presbyterian host church. Many Koreans were interested in participating and integrating into the denomination, but they asked for time to deal with language barriers and customs, such as a suspicion of women ministers. The PC(U.S.A.) fostered a Korean Presbyterian Ministries Committee and also a Korean Language Presbytery. The Reverend Syngman Rhee the Associate Director of the Worldwide Ministries Division served as interpreter of Korean needs and aspirations. Deeply evangelical, Korean Presbyterians promised to invigorate the sharing of the Gospel to the nation and to the world.

Societal and Global Responsibilities

Following the tradition of centuries, Presbyterians continued to deal with what the *Westminster Confession* called "cases of conscience," and to raise the consciousness about challenges Presbyterians faced in the country and around the world. It did this increasingly through denominational studies and reports. These included the "Church's Capacity to Respond to Social, Political, and Economic Crisis" and the "Reformed Faith and Politics," which reviewed Presbyterian history from Calvin's days in Geneva to the 1980s.

Problems came to the General Assembly through resolutions and overtures from individuals, presbyteries, and synods. They were studied by task forces made up of clergy and laity with concerns and expertise on certain matters. Task forces then brought in reports for consideration, adoption, and study by the whole church for stimulation and instruction without binding the conscience. The denomination required that all such studies be rooted in the Bible and supported with theological reflection. These studies may not have been as effective as they were intended because of weakening educational institutions at every level of Christian life.

Presbyterians expressed deep concern for the welfare of the nation and the world. Both the UPCUSA and the PCUS, and then the PC(U.S.A.) in 1983, adopted a program called "Peacemaking: The Believer's Calling," which embraced a quest for wholeness—as the word peacemaking suggests—in all human relations from the family to the nations of the world. In terms of domestic life, the denomination studied domestic violence, sexual exploitation of women, and the abuse of alcohol and drugs. It wrestled with the problems of abortion and homosexuality. With regard to abortion it took a position in "The Covenant of Life and Abortion" (1983) that abortion was never a good option. Under certain circumstances, with pastoral and medical advice, ending a pregnancy may be allowable. With regard to homosexuality, the denomination affirmed the rights of homosexuals as human beings and the church's pastoral concern for all its members, but refused to ordain practicing homosexuals to the ministry. In areas where adherents to the Reformed tradition have been deeply involved in conflict, such as in northern Ireland, South Africa, and the Middle East and Korea because of years of mission work, the denomination urged peace with justice, thus contributing to changes in these, as well as other areas, of the world. The Reverend John M. Fife, pastor of the Southside Presbyterian Church in Tucson, Arizona, joined with other Christians in the "sanctuary movement" to provide a safe haven for Central Americans fleeing the revolutionary turmoils in their countries during the 1970s and 1980s. Fife and others believed this was a compelling "case of conscience" based on the biblical injunction in Lev. 19:33–34, The U.S. government brought criminal charges against them and found them guilty in a nationally watched case. They were running an illegal "underground railroad" for the refugees. In a civil suit, the plaintiffs argued successfully that the government had in "unbridled and inappropriate covert activity" spied on churches, abridging First Amendment liberties.

The denomination also took a look at "Christian Faith and Economic Justice" (1984), a study that dealt with various dimensions of the national and world economy. It called for a people of plenty to devise a system that would provide for all God's people, with an emphasis on self-development. This included healthcare and economic security for children and older adults. The church also continued to explore the Christian responsibility for the earth, and balanced ecological behavior and habits for the good of all God's creatures. At the time of the 200th anniversary of the first General Assembly, it addressed matters of religious liberty, so important in the 1780s, in "God Alone Is Lord of Conscience" (1988). In "Christian Obedience in a Nuclear Age" (1988), it tackled problems of national and global importance. This latter study, performed by a task force headed by the Reverend Albert C. Winn, theologian, former president of Louisville Theological Seminary, and pastor, explored the anxiety of many members. The world still lived under the menace of the "mushroom cloud." The report, stopping short of calling possession of nuclear weapons a sin—a position taken by other Christians—condemned their actual use. It recommended that Christians work for the end of the nuclear arms race. It also called for the continued support and strengthening of the United Nations, to promote a just and durable peace in a nuclear free world. In 1995, Presbyterians remembered their participation in the founding of the United Nations, as the organization observed its fiftieth birthday. The denomination also observed the fortieth anniversary of the Universal Declaration of Human Rights.

These papers and others, dealing not with its own but with the nation's and world's agendas, stirred debate among some Presbyterians, as they were expected to do. Some opposed the reports because they felt the church was *intermeddling* in politics contrary to their interpretation of the *Westminster Confession,* and neglecting religious responsibilities. Others objected to the conclusions of these reports that did not represent the considered membership of the denomination. Still others endorsed these reports as dealing responsibly with complex ethical and moral problems. Through them, Presbyterians dealt with cases of conscience, some of them "cases extraordinary," as indicated in the *Westminster Confession,* and also the *Larger Catechism,* which prohibits "undue silence in a just cause." These debates suggest that Presbyterians, as individuals and as part of the Christian family, have been engaged in a search for the commonwealth. The debate over the proper way to conduct this search, and how the public good should be defined, continued during this period.

Ecumenical Relations
and Interfaith Dialogue

Presbyterians maintained ties to the ecumenical community through the NCC and also the WCC in Geneva. They also continued membership in the Consultation on Church Union, or the Church of Christ Uniting, involving the United Church of Christ, the Episcopal Church, and the United Methodist Church, among others. In 1995 the General Assembly voted that it could not yet officially enter into an ecclesial agreement, and it referred documents on *The COCU Consensus* and *Churches in Covenant Communion* to a committee for study. It wished to clarify for the denomination concerns over the office and role of bishops, of elders, and of ordination services, together with other aspects of the plans.

Presbyterians were also involved in two other ecumenical endeavors. First, the PC(U.S.A.) strongly supported the World Alliance of Reformed Churches, with headquarters in Geneva. According to a report in the 1990s, the Alliance embraced approximately 70 million Christians in 99 countries, in 193 member churches. The world's Reformed family profile looked something like the data presented in the table below. Professor Jane Dempsey Douglass of Princeton Theological Seminary, served as president of the Alliance, with Milan Opocensky of the Czech Republic, served as general secretary.

Continent	Member Churches	Countries
Africa	50	28
Asia	50	14
Caribbean and North America	18	7
Central and South America	21	11
Europe	39	27
Middle East	5	3
Pacific	10	9
Total	193	99

Unfortunately, Presbyterians in the United States of America still lived as a divided Reformed family. In 1989 the largest of these bodies, in addition to the PC(U.S.A.), were the CPC (91,646 members), the Associate

Reformed Presbyterian Church (General Synod; 37,585 members), the Presbyterian Church in America (founded in 1973; 190,160 members), the Korean Presbyterian Church (founded in 1976; 22,000 members), and the Evangelical Presbyterian Church (founded in 1981; 33,000 members).

Moreover, the denomination continued to engage in interfaith dialogue, for mutual understanding and for the welfare of American society, with its growing religious pluralism. It was also concerned for the well-being of the world community. The *Confession of 1967* committed Presbyterians to this effort:

> The Christian finds parallels between other religions and his own and must approach all religions with openness and respect. Repeatedly God has used the insight of non-Christians to challenge the church to renewal. But the reconciling word of the gospel is God's judgement upon all forms of religion, including the Christian. The gift of God in Christ is for all men. The church, therefore, is commissioned to carry the gospel to all men whatever their religion may be and even when they profess none.

In recent years, Presbyterians engaged Jewish and Muslim communities in conversations in this spirit. In the cases of these traditions, Presbyterians dealt with a long history of anti-Semitism, unpleasant to recall. Such dialogue led to self-examination and self-understanding, as well as to an appreciation of other members of God's human family.

When the Presbyterian Church (U.S.A.) was voted into existence in 1983, the General Assembly gave thanks to Almighty God, celebrated the Lord's Supper in Atlanta, Georgia, and dedicated Presbyterians to what it held to be the purpose of all members of the body of Christ, now in a global context. The Plan of Union included in the *Book of Order* a statement from the old UPCNA made in 1925:

> The great ends of the Church are the proclamation of the Gospel for the salvation of humankind; the shelter, nurture and spiritual fellowship of the children of God; the maintenance of divine worship; the preservation of the truth, the promotion of social righteousness: and the exhibition of the Kingdom of Heaven to the world.

In these words, Presbyterians summarized the way they interpreted the challenge of Jesus to his early disciples, and they stated what the church was still called to do at the end of the twentieth century. When the PC(U.S.A.) gathered in 1989 in Philadelphia, where the first General Assembly of the PCUSA had met in 1789, the minutes recorded a total membership of 2,938,830; 11,573 churches; 50,552 male and 69,861 female elders; and 1,109,215 in church schools. The church remembered the promise of God: "Behold, I am making all things new," and called for Presbyterians to live in hope and faith and love.

In the *Brief Statement of Faith*, based on an Apostolic benediction, expressing trust in God the Son, in God the Father, and in God the Spirit, Presbyterians also recognized responsibilities in the world as they moved in hope toward a third millennium in the Common Era:

> We trust in God the Holy Spirit,
>> everywhere the giver and renewer of life.
> The Spirit justifies us by grace through faith,
>> sets us free to accept ourselves and to love God and neighbor,
>> and binds us together with all believers
>> in the one body of Christ, the Church.
> The same Spirit
>> who inspired the prophets and apostles
>> rules our faith and life in Christ through Scripture,
>> engages us through the Word proclaimed,
>> claims us in the waters of baptism,
>> feeds us with the bread of life and the cup of salvation,
>> and calls women and men to all ministries of the Church.
> In a broken and fearful world
> the Spirit gives us courage
>> to pray without ceasing,
>> to witness among all peoples to Christ as Lord and Savior,
>> to unmask idolatries in Church and culture,
>> to hear the voices of peoples long silenced,
>> and to work with others for justice, freedom, and peace.
> In gratitude to God, empowered by the Spirit,
>> we strive to serve Christ in our daily tasks
>>> and to live holy and joyful lives,
>> even as we watch for God's new heaven and new earth,
>>> praying, "Come, Lord Jesus!"
> With believers in every time and place,
>> we rejoice that nothing in life or in death
>> can separate us from the love of God in Christ Jesus our Lord.
> Glory be to the Father, and to the Son, and to the Holy Spirit. Amen.

BIBLIOGRAPHY

American Presbyterians, Journal of Presbyterian History. Philadelphia: Presbyterian Historical Society, 1901.

Armstrong, Maurice W., Lefferts A. Loetscher, and Charles A. Anderson, eds. *The Presbyterian Enterprise: Sources of American Presbyterian History*. Philadelphia: The Westminster Press, 1956.

Bainton, Roland. *Women in the Reformation in France and England*. Minneapolis: Augsburg Publishing House, 1973.

Barrus, Ben M., Milton L. Baughn, and Thomas H. Campbell. *A People Called Cumberland Presbyterians*. Memphis: Frontier Press, 1972.

Boyd, Lois A., and R. Douglas Brackenridge. *Presbyterian Women in America*. Westport, Conn.: Greenwood, 1983.

Brackenridge, R. D., and F. O. Garcia-Treto. *Iglesia Presbiteriana*. San Antonio: Trinity University Press, 1974.

Coalter, Milton J., John W. Mulder, and Louis B. Weeks. *The Re-forming Tradition: Presbyterians and Mainstream Protestanism*. Louisville, Ky.: Westminster/John Knox Press, 1992.

Coleman, Michael. *Presbyterian Missionary Activities Towards American Indians, 1837–1893*. Jackson, Miss.: University Press of Mississippi, 1985..

Hudson, Winthrop S., and John Corrigan. *Religion in America*, 5th ed. New York: Macmillan Publishing Co., 1992.

Jamison, Wallace N. *The United Presbyterian Story: A Centennial Study, 1858–1958*. Pittsburgh: Geneva Press, 1958.

Klett, Guy S., ed. *Minutes of the Presbyterian Church in America, 1706–1788*. Philadelphia: Presbyterian Historical Society, 1976.

Leith, John H. *Introduction to the Reformed Tradition: A Way of Being the Christian Community*, rev. ed. Atlanta: John Knox Press, 1981.

Loetscher, Lefferts A. *The Broadening Church*. Philadelphia: University of Pennsylvania Press, 1954.

McKim, Donald K., ed. *Encyclopedia of the Reformed Faith*. Louisville, Ky.: Westminster/John Knox Press, 1992.

McNeill, John T. *The History and Character of Calvinism*. New York: Oxford University Press, 1954.

McNeill, John T., and James Hastings Nichols. *Ecumenical Testimony*. Philadelphia: Westminster Press, 1974.

Murray, Andrew E. *Presbyterians and the Negro—A History*. Philadelphia: Presbyterian Historical Society, 1966.

Old, Hughes Oliphant. *Worship That Is Reformed According to the Scripture*. Guides to the Reformed Tradition. Atlanta: John Knox Press, 1984.

Presbyterian Church (U.S.A.). *Book of Confessions*. Louisville, Ky.: The Office of the General Assembly, 1991.

————. *Book of Order*. Louisville, Ky.: The Office of the General Assembly, 1992–1993.

————. *Book of Common Worship*. Louisville, Ky: Westminster/John Knox Press, 1993.

Rogers, Jack. *Presbyterian Creeds: A Guide to the Book of Confessions*. Philadelphia: Westminster Press, 1985.

Smylie, James H. ed. "Presbyterians and the American Revolution: An Interpretive Account," *Journal of Presbyterian History* 52 (winter 1974): entire issue.

————.ed. "American Presbyterianism: A Pictorial Account," *Journal of Presbyterian History* 63 (spring/summer 1985): entire issue.

————, ed. "Writings that Have Shaped Our Past," *American Presbyterians* 66 (winter 1988): entire issue.

Stone, Ronald H., ed. *Reformed Faith and Politics*. Washington, D.C.: University Press of America, 1983.

Thompson, Ernest Trice. *Presbyterians in the South*. 3 vols. Atlanta: John Knox Press, 1963–1973.

Trinterud, Leonard John. *The Forming of an American Tradition: A Reexamination of Colonial Presbyterianism*. Philadelphia: The Westminster Press, 1949.

————. *The Presbyterian Hymnal: Hymns, Psalms, and Spiritual Songs*. Louisville, Ky.: Westminster/John Knox Press, 1990.

Wilmore, Gayraud S. *Black and Presbyterian*. Philadelphia: Geneva Press, 1983.

For additional information, please consult the study papers prepared for General Assembly, many of which can be found in the *Minutes of the General Assembly* for various years.

INDEX OF NAMES

INDEX OF SUBJECTS